THE X RESOURCE

ISSUE SIXTEEN

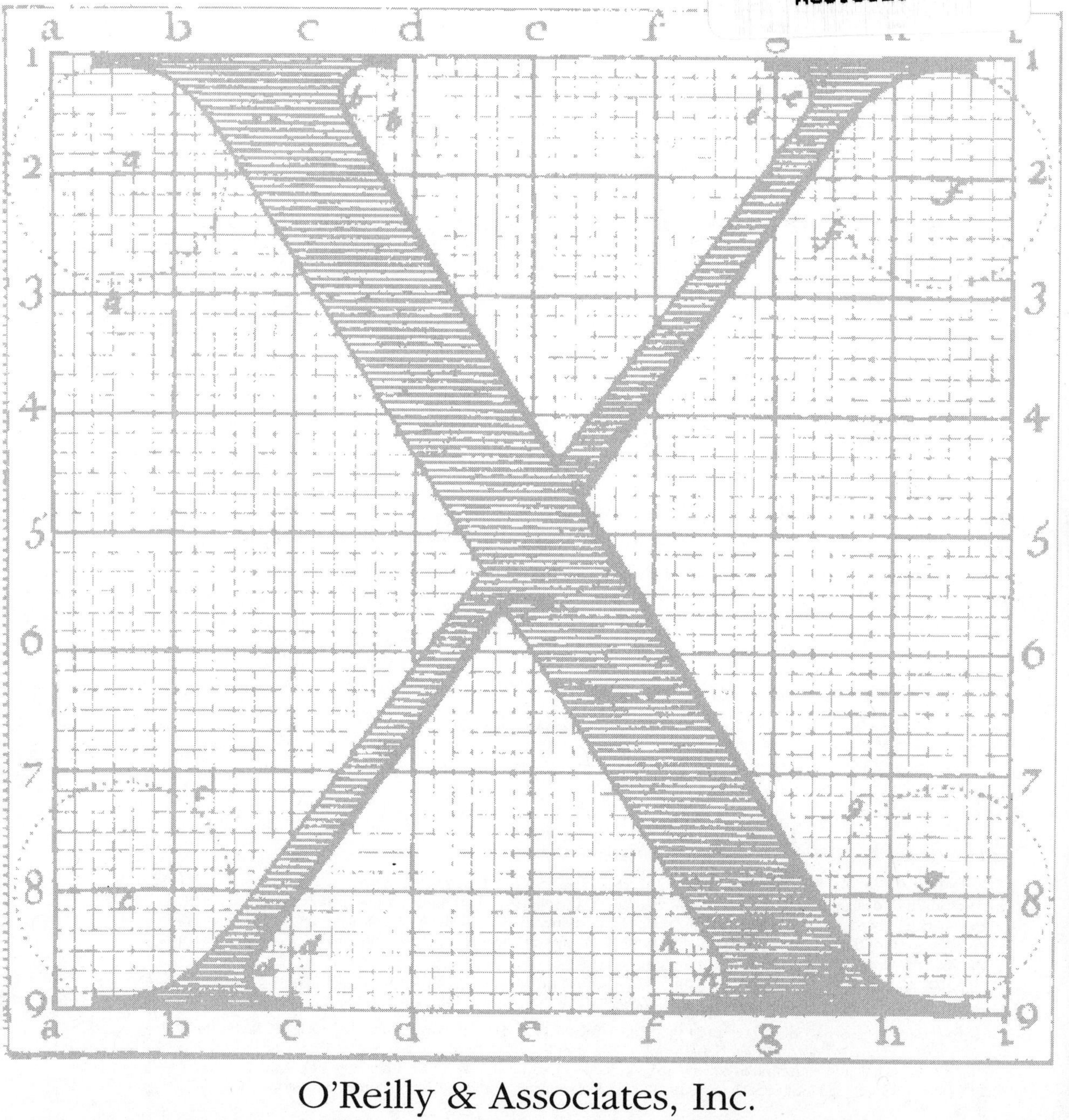

O'Reilly & Associates, Inc.

THE X RESOURCE: A PRACTICAL JOURNAL OF THE X WINDOW SYSTEM
Issue 16, Published December 1995

The X Resource (ISSN 1058-5591) provides timely, in-depth coverage of the issues and techniques in X programming, administration and use. It is published quarterly in January, April, July, and October by O'Reilly & Associates, Inc. The journal is the Official Publisher of the X Consortium's X Technical Conference Proceedings, which form the January issue.

SUBSCRIPTION PRICES (SUBJECT TO CHANGE WITHOUT NOTICE):

Country	Price
USA	$65.00
Canada + Mexico	$70.00
Europe/Africa	$90.00
Asia/Australia	$95.00

Shipping is included in subscription prices, and is via US Postal Service Second Class in the USA, and Air Mail to all foreign addresses.

Single copies of *The X Resource* are available to U.S. and Canadian customers from O'Reilly & Associates, Inc. or from your local bookseller. Customers outside the U.S. and Canada, please inquire at your local bookseller or contact one of our Overseas Distributors listed at the back of this journal.

Payment may be made by check or credit card. Checks should be made out to O'Reilly & Associates, Inc., and must be in U.S. dollars, drawn on a U.S. bank. Foreign customers may call to arrange payment by wire.

CORRESPONDENCE:

Address subscription orders, changes of address, and business correspondence to:

The X Resource
O'Reilly & Associates, Inc.
103 Morris Street, Suite A
Sebastopol, CA 95472
(800) 998-9938 *USA/Canada* • (707) 829-0515 *Overseas or Local* • (707) 829-0104 *FAX*

Editorial correspondence (including requests for permission to reproduce material from *The X Resource*) should be addressed to:

The X Resource
c/o Paula M. Ferguson
1630 30th St., #210
Boulder, CO 80301

electronic mail: *paula@ora.com* or *uunet!ora!paula*

Printed on
Recycled
Paper

A PRACTICAL JOURNAL OF THE X WINDOW SYSTEM

THE X RESOURCE

TABLE OF CONTENTS

ISSUE SIXTEEN

THE X RESOURCE: A PRACTICAL JOURNAL OF THE X WINDOW SYSTEM

O'Reilly & Associates, Inc.

The Official Publisher of the
X Consortium's X Technical Conference Proceedings.

PUBLISHER

Tim O'Reilly

MANAGING EDITOR

Frank Willison
(O'Reilly & Associates, Inc.)

EDITOR

Paula M. Ferguson
(O'Reilly & Associates, Inc.)

EDITORIAL ADVISORY BOARD

Jeff Barr (Vertex Software, Inc.)
Todd Brunhoff (North Valley Research)
Kevin Calhoun (Informix Software)
Ellis Cohen (Open Software Foundation)
Wayne Dyksen (Dept. of Computer Science, Purdue University)
Jim Fulton (Network Computing Devices, Inc.)
Ronald Hughes (CrossWind Technologies, Inc.)
Bob Joyce (Aspect, Inc.)
Phil Karlton (Silicon Graphics, Inc.)
John Buford (University of Massachusetts—Lowell)
Mark Linton (Silicon Graphics, Inc.)
Stuart Marks (Sun Microsystems)
Chris Peterson (Investment Management Services, Inc.)
Bob Scheifler with the staff (X Consortium) (acting as a single board member)

CUSTOMER SERVICE AND ADMINISTRATION

Marianne Cooke

COPY EDITING

Nancy Crumpton

COVER AND INTERIOR FORMAT DESIGN

Edie Freedman

PRODUCTION

Mike Sierra

ILLUSTRATIONS

Chris Reilley

FROM THE EDITOR

This issue closes our fourth year of publishing *THE X RESOURCE*. I hope that you continue to find the information that we provide useful and interesting.

I am also excited to let you know that O'Reilly & Associates is going to be publishing another quarterly journal, the *World Wide Web Journal*. The Web Consortium (W3C), headed by Tim Berners-Lee, is the official standards body for the Web. The *World Wide Web Journal* will provide timely, in-depth coverage of the W3C's technological developments, such as protocols for security, replication and caching, HTML and SGML, and content labeling. It will also explore the broader issues of the Web with interviews with Web luminaries and articles on controversial legal issues such as censorship and intellectual property rights.

The *World Wide Web Journal* will be published quarterly in January, April, July, and October. The first issue of the journal will contain the Conference Proceedings papers that were chosen for the 4th International World Wide Web conference in Boston, Massachusetts. If you want to keep up with the state of the Web, check out this new journal.

HIGHLIGHTS OF THIS ISSUE

This issue begins with an article on implementing an online help system for X/Motif applications using a Web browser like Netscape or Mosaic. With the increasing popularity of the Web, this is certainly a viable approach for providing online help. The author explains how to take advantage of the remote control features of these browsers using the XtscHelp toolkit. The author designed this toolkit to make it easy to use a Web browser for an online help system.

In the next article, Douglas Rand describes the GoldenGate and MediaWarehouse projects. These systems are designed to facilitate the use of digital media on Silicon Graphics platforms. They address the important issues of moving data between different software programs and providing long-term storage for digital media. As the use of images, audio files, and movies continues to increase, these issues will need to be solved.

The next paper discusses a technique for visualizing the network performance of X applications. The author was faced with analyzing problems with the start-up performance of an X application running over the Internet. Using the technique that he developed, the author was able to gain insight into why certain types of behavior can be problematic when an X application is being used over the Internet.

The final paper describes the implementation of the PanoramiX Extension, the Digital solution for a multi-headed environment. This extension provides a way for a multi-headed system to function as one large screen. Windows can span multiple screens and can move from one screen to another.

In the Documentation section, we begin with a tutorial on Java, the new programming language being developed by Sun. Everyone seems to be talking about Java, so we wanted to give you a brief introduction to what it's all about.

Finally, we provide a tutorial on the X Synchronization Extension, XSync. The tutorial describes the purpose of the extension and the concepts involved before providing some examples of its use. This tutorial and the accompanying reference pages are an excerpt from the forthcoming *X Programmer's Handbook*, Volume 9 in O'Reilly's X Window System series.

NEXT ISSUE: X TECHNICAL CONFERENCE

The 10th Annual X Technical Conference will be held on February 12 -14, 1996, at the Fairmont Hotel in San Jose, California. The next issue of *THE X RESOURCE* will comprise the proceedings of the conference.

Enjoy the issue.

Paula M. Ferguson
Editor

10TH ANNUAL X TECHNICAL CONFERENCE

XTECH'96
10th Annual X Technical Conference
Fairmont Hotel, San Jose, CA
12-14 February 1996

Sponsored by X Consortium, Inc.

Full conference information, including tutorial abstracts, registration form, hotel reservation form, and airline discounts, is available on the Web at *http://www.x.org/consortium/conf.html*. You can also request a copy by sending email to *xconference@x.org*.

CONFERENCE FORMAT

The entire conference will be held at the Fairmont Hotel in San Jose, CA. There are no vendor exhibits.

Monday, 12 February 1996
    Tutorials & Birds-Of-A-Feather Sessions

Tuesday, 13 February
    Talks & Reception

Wednesday, 14 February
    Talks & Birds-Of-A-Feather Sessions

PRE-REGISTRATION

The pre-registration fee is $350 per person. The pre-registration fee for full-time students only is discounted to $175. Pre-registrations must be received by 15 January 1996 to qualify for these fees.

ON-SITE REGISTRATION (SPACE-AVAILABLE BASIS)

The on-site registration fee is $450 per person. There is no discounted on-site student registration fee. On-site registration will take place at the Fairmont Hotel at the following times:

Sunday, 11 February 1996	3:00 pm - 8:00 pm
Monday, 12 February	7:30 am - 4:00 pm
Tuesday, 13 February	7:30 am - 4:00 pm

HOTEL ACCOMODATIONS

The Fairmont Hotel has reserved a block of rooms for conference participants from Saturday, 10 February, through Friday, 16 February 1996. The hotel features five restaurants, health club facilities including a rooftop swimming pool, and a business center.

Conference rate: $125/night for a single room, $135/night for a double room, exclusive of a 10% tax/night.

Questions regarding hotel accommodations should be directed to the Fairmont Hotel, Tel: 408-998-1900 or 800-527-4727.

TUTORIALS

The following tutorials will be given on Monday, 12 February:

CDE Desktop KornShell Programming Techniques
    J. Stephen Pendergrast, Jr., Novell, Inc.

Introduction to Rapid Application Development using OpenStep(tm) on X11/DPS
    Laurence P. G. Cable, OpenStep Development Group, Object Products, SunSoft, Inc.

Developing Internationalized GUI Applications
    Thomas C. McFarland, Hewlett-Packard Co.

Programming with OpenGL: An Introduction
    Paula Womack, Silicon Graphics, Inc.

Using Threads with Today's Motif
    Dave Hill, Digital Equipment Corp.

Writing Rugged GUI Tests
    Sankar L. Chakrabarti, Hewlett-Packard Co.
    Rajeev Pandey, Hewlett-Packard Co.
    Sami Mohammed, X Consortium, Inc.

Using the X Image Extension: Programming with XIElib
    Syd Logan, Senior Software Engineer, AGE Logic, Inc.

Creating Your Own Corporate Style Guide
    Laura A. Bryant, New Technology, Inc.

Advanced OpenGL with the X Window System
    Mark J. Kilgard, Silicon Graphics, Inc.

The Power of the CDE Help System: How You Can Make Your Application Sing and Dance
    Lori A. Cook, Workstation Technology Center, Hewlett-Packard Co.
    Tracy Porter, RISC System/6000 Division, IBM Corp.
    Douglas C. Woestendiek, RISC System/6000 Division, IBM Corp.

GUI Programming in Java
    Jan Newmarch, University of Canberra

Managing Graphical Interfaces in an Heterogeneous Environment
    Alex Robinson, Senior System Engineer, SAIC Ltd.

TALKS

The following talks are currently scheduled for Tuesday, 13 February:

Dynamic Extension and Control of Xt Applications
    Jan Newmarch, Huimin Xu, University of Canberra

SCO Visual Tcl: An Introspective Look
    Mary Toscano, Senior Software Engineer, The Santa Cruz Operation (SCO)

Developing MT-hot Motif applications and MT-safe Motif widgets
    John Mani, Member of Technical Staff, Motif group, SunSoft, Inc.
    Kapono Carter, Member of Technical Staff, Motif group, SunSoft, Inc.

Xt Components: An Alternative to Writing Compound Widgets
    David K. Bainbridge, Integrated Computer Solutions, Inc.

You Can Print From X! (Part II)
    Axel Deininger, Workstation Technology Center, Hewlett-Packard Co.

Å(awe), an interpreted language for interactive animations
    Gunnar Rønning, Svein Johansen, Kjell Øystein Arisland
    Department of Informatics, University of Oslo

HBX: High-Bandwidth X for Satellite Internetworking
    Yongguang Zhang, Son Dao, Hughes Research Laboratories

NTrigue: Networking NT applications using X
    Keith Packard, Network Computing Devices, Inc.

Broadway: Universal Access to Interactive Applications over the Web
    Bob Scheifler, X Consortium, Inc.

Building the Interactive Web Using X
  Kaleb S. Keithley, X Consortium, Inc.

The Broadway Audio System
  Ray Tice, Mark Welch, X Consortium, Inc.

Security Architecture for Broadway
  Stephen Gildea, X Consortium, Inc.

The following talks are currently scheduled for Wednesday, 14 February:

Secure Application Sharing under X
  Dr. Oliver Pfaff, Siemens AG

Trusted CDE
  Glen Faden, Sun Microsystems Federal

XMovie: Application Services for Distributed Multimedia Systems
  Ralf Keller, Praktische Informatik IV, University of Mannheim

X Multimedia Services and Infrastructure
  Mike Patnode, SCO Senior Member of Technical Staff, X Consortium Guest Staff

The MediaWarehouse - Integrating Multimedia Data through X
  Kenton Lee, Consultant, Silicon Graphics, Inc.

Dynamic loadable architecture for X library internationalization
  Shinobu Matsuzuka, Hidetoshi Tajima, Alexander Gelfenbain, SunSoft, Inc.

GLR, an OpenGL render server facility
  Mark J. Kilgard, Silicon Graphics, Inc.

WidgetLint - A run time GUI debugger
  Ido Sarig, Software Manager, Mercury Interactive

Testing "Internationalized" GUI Applications
  Sankar L. Chakrabarti, Hewlett-Packard Co.
  Sunil Girdhar, HCL Hewlett-Packard Ltd.

Enhancing Testability of X Clients
  Sami Mohammed, X Consortium, Inc.
  Shankar Chakrabarti, Hewlett-Packard Co.

RECORD: An extension for X protocol capture
  David P. Wiggins, X Consortium, Inc.

BOFS

The following birds of a feather sessions are currently planned. We welcome suggestions for additional BOFS; send suggestions to *xconference@x.org*.

OpenGL and X
    Mark J. Kilgard, Silicon Graphics, Inc.

Creating Shrink-Wrapped X Applications on SVR4
    Stuart Anderson, Metro Link, Inc.

The X Print Server
    Axel Deininger, Workstation Technology Center, Hewlett-Packard Co.

OBTAINING THE SOURCE CODE

The source code for all public-domain and free software that is discussed in the X Resource is available electronically in a number of ways: by *ftp*, *ftpmail*, *bitftp*, and *uucp*. The cheapest, fastest, and easiest ways to get it are listed first. If you read from the top down, the first one that works for you is probably the best. Use *ftp* if you are directly on the Internet. Use *ftpmail* if you are not on the Internet but can send and receive electronic mail to internet sites (this includes CompuServe users). Use BITFTP if you send electronic mail via BITNET. Use *uucp* if none of the above works.

FTP

To use *ftp*, you need a machine with direct access to the Internet. A sample session is shown, with what you should type in boldface.

```
% ftp ftp.uu.net
Connected to ftp.uu.net.
220 FTP server (Version 6.21 Tue Mar 10 22:09:55 EST 1992) ready.
Name (ftp.uu.net:sierra): anonymous
331 Guest login ok, send domain style e-mail address as password.
Password: sierra@ora.com (use your user name and host here)
230 Guest login ok, access restrictions apply.
ftp> cd /published/oreilly/xresource/issue16
250 CWD command successful.
ftp> binary (Very important! You must specify binary transfer for compressed files.)
200 Type set to I.
ftp> get filename
200 PORT command successful.
150 Opening BINARY mode data connection for FILE.
226 Transfer complete.
ftp> quit
221 Goodbye.
%
```

The following example is for compressed *tar* archives. If the file is a compressed *tar* archive, extract the files from the archive by typing:

```
% zcat FILE.tar.Z | tar xf -
```

System V systems require the following *tar* command instead:

```
% zcat FILE.tar.Z | tar xof -
```

If *zcat* is not available on your system, use separate *uncompress* and *tar* commands.

If the file is a compressed *shar* archive, you can extract the files from the archive by typing:

```
% uncompress FILE.shar.Z
% /bin/sh FILE.shar
```

FTPMAIL

FTPMAIL is a mail server available to anyone who can send and receive electronic mail to and from Internet sites. This includes most workstations that have an email connection to the outside world, and CompuServe users. You do not need to be directly on the Internet. Here's how to do it.

You send mail to *ftpmail@decwrl.dec.com*. In the message body, give the name of the anonymous *ftp* host and the *ftp* commands you want to run. The server will run anonymous *ftp* for you and mail the files back to you. To get a complete help file, send a message with no subject and the single word "help" in the body. The following is an example mail session that should get you the examples. This command sends you a listing of the files in the selected directory, and the requested examples file. The listing is useful in case there's a later version of the examples you're interested in.

```
% mail ftpmail@decwrl.dec.com
Subject:
reply jerry@ora.com          (where you want files mailed)
connect ftp.uu.net
chdir /published/oreilly/xresource/issue16
dir
binary
uuencode                     (or btoa if you have it)
get filename
quit
%
```

A signature at the end of the message is acceptable as long as it appears after "quit."

All retrieved files will be split into 60KB chunks and mailed to you. You then remove the mail headers and concatenate them into one file, and then *uudecode* or *btoa* it. Once you've got the desired file, follow the directions under *ftp* to extract the files from the archive.

VMS, DOS, and Mac versions of *uudecode, btoa, uncompress,* and *tar* are available. The VMS versions are on *gatekeeper.dec.com* in */archive/pub/VMS*.

BITFTP

BITFTP is a mail server for BITNET users. You send it electronic mail messages requesting files, and it sends you back the files by electronic mail. BITFTP currently serves only users who send it mail from nodes that are directly on BITNET/EARN/NetNorth. BITFTP is a public service of Princeton University. Here's how it works.

To use BITFTP, send mail containing your *ftp* commands to *BITFTP@PUCC*. For a complete help file, send HELP as the message body.

The following is the message body you should send to BITFTP:

```
FTP  ftp.uu.net  NETDATA
USER  anonymous
PASS your Internet email address (not your bitnet address)
CD  /published/oreilly/xresource/issue16
DIR
BINARY
GET filename
QUIT
```

Once you've got the desired file, follow the directions under *ftp* to extract the files from the archive. Since you are probably not on a UNIX system, you may need to get versions of *uudecode, uncompress, btoa,* and *tar* for your system. VMS, DOS, and Mac versions are available. The VMS versions are on gatekeeper.dec.com in */archive/pub/VMS*.

Questions about BITFTP can be directed to Melinda Varian, *MAINT@PUCC* on BITNET.

UUCP

uucp is standard on virtually all UNIX systems, and is available for IBM-compatible PCs and Apple Macintoshes. The examples are available by *uucp* via modem from UUNET; UUNET's connect-time charges apply.

You can get the examples from UUNET whether you have an account or not. If you or your company has an account with UUNET, you will have a system with a direct *uucp* connection to UUNET. Find that system, and type:

```
% uucp  uunet\!~/published/oreilly/xresource/issue16/filename
yourhost\!~/yourname/
```

The backslashes can be omitted if you use the Bourne shell (sh) instead of csh. The file should appear some time later (up to a day or more) in the directory */usr/spool/uucp-public/yourname*. If you don't have an account but would like one so that you can get electronic mail, then contact UUNET at 703-204-8000.

If you don't have a UUNET account, you can set up a *uucp* connection to UUNET using the phone number 1-900-468-7727. As of this writing, the cost is 50 cents per minute. The charges will appear on your next telephone bill. The login name is "uucp" with no password. For example, an L.sys/Systems entry might look like:

```
uunet Any ACU 19200 1-900-468-7727 ogin:--ogin: uucp
```

Your entry may vary depending on your *uucp* configuration. If you have a PEP-capable modem, make sure s50=255s111=30 is set before calling.

It's a good idea to get the file */published/oreilly/xresource/ls-lR.Z* as a short test file containing the filenames and sizes of all the files in the directory.

Once you've got the desired file, follow the directions under *ftp* to extract the files from the archive.

PAPERS

An Elegant Online Help System for X/Motif Programs

GoldenGate: Automatic Conversion and the MediaWarehouse

Visualizing X Window System Performance

The PanoramiX Extension

An Elegant Online Help System for X/Motif Programs

Keith Gemeinhart

Abstract

Implementing an online help system is no longer a luxury; it is a necessity. Users expect some type of online help or documentation with a quality application, and you as a programmer must provide it. Unfortunately, when time and money are budgeted for a project, online help becomes an afterthought. As a software developer you must reconcile the expectations of the user with the demands of the project manager.

Currently, the X/Motif programming community lacks a portable, high-quality, low-cost solution for providing online help. Combining the remote control features of a World Wide Web (WWW) browser such as Netscape or NCSA Mosaic with some simple callback procedures fills this void elegantly.

With this in mind, I have designed the XtscHelp toolkit. It is an interface between an X/Motif program and a WWW browser, allowing you to use the browser for your online help system.

*Keith Gemeinhart (**keithg@tsc.com**) is a software engineer working for the computer software and services group of Technology Service Corporation in Bloomington, Indiana.*

The X Resource • Issue 16

19

INTRODUCTION

Designing and implementing a help system consisting of dialog boxes is relatively simple. Still, many programmers and users crave a more powerful online help system. Creating such a system from scratch, however, is not simple. Additionally, programmers often face the task of porting their work to many different platforms. Manipulating graphics and text, the main elements of a help system, are two of the more difficult concepts for an X/Motif programmer to master, let alone port.

In this paper, I describe the rationale for using a WWW browser as the vehicle for an online help system. Next, I explain the remote control APIs for Netscape and Mosaic that make this possible. Finally, I describe the XtscHelp toolkit, which I designed to make it easy to use a Web browser for your online help system. I include information on how to use the toolkit, as well as some of its implementation details.

OK, BUT WHY USE A WEB BROWSER?

Since a well-understood and well-liked interface provides the highest quality help system, Web browsers are a natural choice. In less than two years, these browsers have helped transform the Web into the hottest mainstream business and information medium available. Fortunately, mechanisms exist to harness their power for use in an online help system.

Even though many commercial and public domain help systems are available, none have the features that satisfy the end user and the developer as well as Web browsers do. No other system can be integrated so frugally. In short, this solution satisfies the user and the project manager while providing features that no other help system can match.

SATISFYING THE USER

A primary goal when designing an application is providing the user with a comfortable, useful, and well-designed interface. The characteristics most visible to the user are its ability to be customized, ease of use, and available features.

Two users rarely use an application the same way. Allowing customization increases productivity and reduces frustration. The user can easily add documents associated with your application's problem domain [Shneiderman92]. In addition, the application defaults files allow customization of color, font, and keystroke resources, as well as many others.

If a help system's interface is not easy to use, it is not effective. That is, a poorly designed interface hinders the user more than it helps. Furthermore, a short learning curve reduces training time, and easily reversible actions facilitate exploration of the content. Navigating through a set of documents with a Web browser is simple: point and click. Highlighted text progressively guides the user to more detailed information. Back and forward buttons encourage users to freely explore the help content without getting lost because they can easily reverse their actions.

Providing a help system that only displays the documentation may not always be enough for the user. Users like to do things that are often difficult to implement such as printing a document containing graphics and text or seeing a history of the documents they have read. Web browsers allow PostScript printing. Additionally, the following features are already built-in: email, bookmarks, history, annotations (Mosaic only), multiple simultaneous windows, and on-page searching. All of these traits make Web browsers a worthy solution from the user's perspective.

SATISFYING THE PROJECT MANAGER

The end user may never get a chance to use your application or its help system if it never gets delivered. Satisfying your project manager with short development time and an inexpensive, portable help system ensures that your application (and its help system) will make it out the door.

The development and testing of new code takes a great deal of time. Less code to write and test means less development time spent on the help system. When developing the XtscHelp toolkit, I designed callbacks that are easy to integrate because a good help system integrates easily into an existing application. Furthermore, the toolkit requires very little testing because of its simplicity. This allows you to spend more of your budgeted time developing and testing your application.

Buying new widgets can be expensive. With some help widgets, run-time licensing, help text compilers, and site licensing can add to the cost. The browsers themselves are inexpensive. Netscape costs about $40 per copy, and Mosaic is free. Packaging these products with your application, however, requires negotiating with the respective developers. A typical solution would require the end user to obtain one of the browsers as a requirement for viewing online documentation.

Few products today run on only a single platform. Consequently, providing consistent operation and a universal look and feel on all platforms is important. Netscape and Mosaic are both available for all major UNIX platforms. Again, I designed the callback interface functions with simplicity in mind to limit the need for platform-specific code. This, in turn, increases its portability.

These traits make Web browsers a worthy solution from the project manager's perspective.

FEATURES EVERYONE WILL LOVE

Printed documentation rarely contains only text. Online documentation should not be one-dimensional either. Furthermore, if it is difficult to produce the help content, you may not be able to utilize all of your help system's capabilities. The rapidly evolving HTML language makes it easy to produce richly formatted help documents. Some features supported by HTML and the Web browsers include images (GIF, JPEG, and XPM formats), tables, and numerous text formatting commands. Fortunately, the same explosive Internet growth that spawned Netscape and Mosaic has also produced an abundance of HTML editors. Excellent commercial and public domain authoring tools are available. These can help you produce high-quality content for your online help system.

If everyone communicated in the same language, developers could write their applications for a single audience. Since we want our applications to reach the widest possible audience, we must consider internationalization. A key to successful internationalization is isolating the text from the compiled code. Since the WWW browsers read their text at runtime from ASCII files, writing a separate set of help files for each locale provides a means for internationalization. Again, HTML authoring tools make this easier.

WWW browsers also have a feature that no other help system can match—they provide direct access to Internet services such as Gopher, Telnet, FTP, and Usenet news. These services can be used as secondary help sources by providing links to related information.

If both the user and developer have Internet connections, you can utilize the browser's client/server features. A combination of local help documents at the user's site and remote documents at the developer's site can be provided transparently. Such an arrangement allows the developer to exploit a Web browser's ability to transfer files and work with interactive forms. Forms enable the user to give feedback, submit bug reports, or ask questions. The file transfer mechanism allows distribution of software updates, help text updates, and release notes. A browser's firewall support and secure transaction mechanisms (available in Netscape only) could also prove useful when exchanging sensitive information.

Finally, imagine the impact of adding clickable images and sound or video clips to an online tutorial. Both Netscape and Mosaic use the MIME standard for supporting helper applications to handle multimedia elements embedded in documents.

These features, accompanied by the widespread use and intuitive nature of Web browsers, makes them a natural choice for use in an online help system.

NETSCAPE'S REMOTE CONTROL API

Displaying a document remotely with a Netscape browser is a simple procedure. The mechanism operates on an already running Netscape process. Remote control is initiated by re-issuing the *netscape* command using the command-line switch *-remote* followed by an action and optional arguments to that action [Zawinski95]. For example, to open a new URL by remote control, issue a command similar to:

```
netscape -remote 'openURL(http://www.tsc.com/)'
```

This causes the Netscape process that is currently running to retrieve and display the document at the specified URL, in this case, the Technology Service Corporation home page.

Examining this command more closely provides a better understanding of each of the elements. *netscape* is the command that normally starts a new Netscape process. Since it is followed by the *-remote* switch, it connects instead to a Netscape process that is already running. `openURL()` is the action being performed, and `"http://www.tsc.com/"` is the argument to that action.

The actions you can perform share their names with Netscape's Xt resource names. Therefore, you can easily map menu items to action names by examining Netscape's application defaults file, *Netscape.ad*. The **Open URL** menu item, for example, corresponds to the resource openURL.

To use the remote control feature, the action must be executed on a display running a Netscape browser version 1.1 or higher. However, it does not have to be running on the same host as your Motif program because X Window System properties are the underlying remote control mechanism. If a Netscape browser is not running on the display, the action fails. A failed attempt results in the following error message, printed to standard error:

```
netscape: not running on display keithg:0.0
```

Where *keithg:0.0* is the name of the display.

NCSA MOSAIC'S REMOTE CONTROL API

Displaying a document using Mosaic's API is a bit more complicated because its remote control takes place via the NCSA's Common Client Interface (CCI) library. The library is written in C and is freely available for programmers creating software that communicates with Mosaic [NCSA95]. The CCI library consists of a set of routines for creating and using a TCP/IP connection between Mosaic and its client program.

The CCI library is available as a self-extracting shell archive from the following URL:

```
ftp://ftp.ncsa.uiuc.edu/Mosaic/CCI/Unix/libcci.src.shar
```

You have to obtain and compile this library to use the Mosaic remote control API. Information on using the CCI library is provided in Thompson95.

THE CCI PORT

Before requesting any URLs, you must establish a CCI connection between the client program and Mosaic. The connection is made through TCP/IP sockets on a dedicated port. Obviously, both Mosaic and the application controlling it must agree on the port. Any unused port between 1024 and 65535 is valid. Mosaic listens on this port for incoming CCI data sent by a client. You can configure the port number from Mosaic's **File** menu, from the command line, or in a resource file. Since the connection is made through TCP/IP sockets, CCI requires that both Mosaic and the client program know on which port communication will take place.

MCCICONNECT

The first step in creating a CCI connection is initialization. A client initializes the library by calling MCCIInitialize(). Next, the client creates a CCI connection by calling MCCI-Connect(). The prototype for this function follows:

```
MCCIPort MCCIConnect( char *serverAddress, int port,
                      void (*callBack)(), void *callBackData );
```

serverAddress is the hostname or IP address on which Mosaic is running. Since Mosaic is a WWW client, the name *serverAddress* may seem like a misnomer. The name is actually correct because Mosaic acts as a server for CCI requests. `port` is the TCP/IP port on which the CCI communication takes place. If this function returns a non-NULL value, the client has successfully established a connection.

MCCIGet

Once a connection has been established, the client displays a document by calling either `MCCIGet()` or `MCCINBGet()`. These functions are identical except that `MCCINBGet()` does not block while Mosaic is getting the requested URL.

For example, to open a new URL by remote control, make a call similar to the following:

```
MCCIGet (cci_port, "http://www.tsc.com/", MCCI_DEFAULT, MCCI_ABSOLUTE,
        NULL);
```

This causes the Mosaic process that is currently running to retrieve and display the document at the specified URL, in this case, the Technology Service Corporation home page.

Examining this function call more closely provides a better understanding of each of the elements. `cci_port` describes the CCI connection. It is the value returned by MCCIConnect(). Again, *http://www.tsc.com/* is the URL of the document. `MCCI_DEFAULT` tells Mosaic how to handle the request. The other possible values are:

MCCI_OUTPUT_CURRENT
    Use the current window to display the document.

MCCI_OUTPUT_NEW
    Open a new window to display the document.

MCCI_OUTPUT_NONE
    Do not display the document.

MCCI_DEFAULT
    Same as `MCCI_OUTPUT_CURRENT`.

MCCI_ABSOLUTE indicates whether the URL should be an absolute or relative hyperlink. Possible values are:

MCCI_ABSOLUTE

MCCI_RELATIVE

MCCI_DEFAULT
    Same as `MCCI_ABSOLUTE`.

The final argument, NULL, indicates that no additional header information should be passed to the HTTP server.

Mosaic version 2.5 or higher must be running on the same host as the client program. If a Mosaic browser is not running, the request fails. If `MCCIGet()` is successful, it returns a value of `MCCI_OK`, and if it fails, the result is `MCCI_FAIL`.

USING THE XTSCHELP TOOLKIT

The XtscHelp toolkit implements the remote control features of Mosaic and Netscape through callbacks for X/Motif programs. As noted earlier, the driving factors in designing and implementing the toolkit were low cost and portability without sacrificing quality. Its simplicity makes meeting these requirements possible.

The latest version of the XtscHelp toolkit is freely available via anonymous FTP at the following address:

```
ftp://ftp.tsc.com/pub/tools/XtscHelp.tar.gz
```

To use the toolkit, compile *XtscHelp.c* as you would any other ANSI-C, Motif program. Then link the resulting object file with the rest of your application's object files. Your application should also include the *XtscHelp.h* header file. If desired, you can compile only the Netscape-relative portion of the toolkit by defining `NO_CCI_SUPPORT` at compile time.

FUNCTION CALLS

The one primary public function is `XtscHelpCallback()`. It takes a URL as its client data and requests that the document be displayed on either a Netscape or Mosaic browser. Three other functions, `XtscHelpLocalCallback()`, `XtscHelpRemote-Callback()`, and `XtscHelpCwdCallback()`, provide the convenience of shorter URLs. They display documents exclusively on the local machine, exclusively on a remote server, or relative to the current working directory (cwd), respectively. The first call to any of these callbacks starts a browser and displays the requested document. All subsequent invocations of the callbacks then update that browser.

You can attach on of the XtscHelp callbacks to a widget with a call similar to the following:

```
XtAddCallback (helpButton1, XmNactivateCallback,
               (XtCallbackProc) XtscHelpCallback,
               (XtPointer) "http://www.tsc.com/css" );
```

The result is a call to `XtscHelpCallback()` with an argument of `"http://www.tsc.com/css"` when the user clicks `helpButton1`. You can provide context-sensitive help by using `XmNhelpCallback` instead of `XmNactivateCallback`.

XTSCHELPCALLBACK

This function is the heart of the toolkit. It takes any valid URL as its client data argument and requests that the document be displayed on either a Netscape or Mosaic browser. The variable `using_netscape_` determines which browser is used. This variable is global to the *XtscHelp.c* module and is declared `extern` in *XtscHelp.h*. If it is set to `True`, a Netscape browser displays the documents. Otherwise, a Mosaic browser handles the help files. By setting this variable in your application, you can dynamically choose the browser. Changing it via a set of toggle buttons allows the user to make the decision.

XTSCHELPREMOTECALLBACK

This function requests a URL from a predetermined remote server. The path of the requested document should be passed as the client data. The protocol specification (*http://*) and server name are prepended to it. You can set the server name through the `XTSC_REMOTE_SERVER` definition in *XtscHelp.c*.

If, for example, you have many requests to the Technology Service Corporation server, define `XTSC_REMOTE_SERVER` as "`www.tsc.com`". Then, to request the URL *http://www.tsc.com/css/people.html*, use `XtscHelpRemoteCallback()` with an argument of "`css/people.html`".

XTSCHELPLOCALCALLBACK

This function requests a URL on the local machine. It is useful if you are accessing files rather than querying a Web server. A fully qualified path should be passed as the client data. This function converts the client data into a valid URL by prepending *file:*. Therefore, to request the file */home/projects/helptext.html* from the machine running your application, use `XtscHelpLocalCallback()` with an argument of "`/home/projects/help-text.html`".

XTSCHELPCWDCALLBACK

Similarly, this function requests files that are on the local server relative to the current working directory. A relative path should be passed as the client data. It is useful if all of your help files are in a single directory tree. It converts a relative path into a valid URL by prepending *file:* and the current working directory. Therefore, to request the file *./helpfiles/index.html* you could use `XtscHelpLocalCallback()` with an argument of "`help-files/index.html`".

SETTING THE CCI PORT

As discussed earlier, Mosaic and its client must agree on a common communication port. The port number is usually specified in Mosaic's application defaults file or as a command-line argument. Making sure that Mosaic and its client are communicating on the same port is vital. Therefore, I chose to configure the CCI port programmatically rather than depend on a user setting the value correctly. Since the first invocation of an XtscHelp callback starts a browser, I specify the CCI port at that point.

You can set the port number by defining `XTSC_MOSAIC_PORT` in *XtscHelp.c*. Check with your system administrator to verify that the port you choose is not already assigned to another service.

Toolkit Implementation Details

The basic implementation of the XtscHelp toolkit is not too complicated. All of the specialized callbacks eventually call `XtscHelpCallback()`. This routine checks the value of `using_netscape_` and then takes the necessary actions for the browser in use. I provide this variable as a mechanism for programmatically determining which browser to use.

Netscape

The Netscape API can be implemented easily in C simply by building the desired command string and executing it through a `system` call. The function `XtscNetscapeURL()` does exactly this. This function is called by `XtscHelpCallback()` if `using_netscape_` is `True`. It is implemented as follows:

```
...
#define XTSC_NETSCAPE_URL "netscape -remote 'openURL(%s)' &"
...

static void XtscNetscapeURL( const char *full_url )
{
  char *command;
  int status;
  static int tries=0;

  command = (char *) XtMalloc (strlen (XTSC_NETSCAPE_URL) +
                               strlen (full_url) + 1);

  sprintf (command, XTSC_NETSCAPE_URL, full_url );

  status = system (command );

  XtFree (command );

  if (status !=0 && tries < XTSC_HELP_MAX_TRIES )
  {
    XtscNetscapeStart ();

    tries++;
    XtscNetscapeURL (full_url );

    sleep (1);
    return;
```

```
      }

      if (status !=0 && tries >= XTSC_HELP_MAX_TRIES )
          XtscHelpError ("Cannot start Netscape !" ); }
```

The command is built using the **XTSC_NETSCAPE_URL** definition and the URL of the document to be displayed. The ampersand (&) allows the command to be executed in the background, so that control is returned immediately to your X program. If it was executed without being run in the background, no X events could be processed until the **system** command returned.

MOSAIC

The **XtscMosaicIntialize()** function takes care of the overhead. It starts the browser and initializes the TCP/IP connection with that process, as shown below:

```
      static MCCIPort XtscMosaicInitialize( Widget w )
      {
        MCCIPort mcci_port;
        char *server_address;
        int port;
        static int tries=0;

        /* Determine the port on which Mosaic should listen for */
        port = XtscMosaicGetPort( w );

        /* Start the Mosaic browser ... */
        XtscMosaicStart(port);

        /* Initialize the CCI library. */
        MCCIInitialize();

        /* Get the hostname  */
        server_address = XtscGetServerAddress();

        /* Make the CCI connection */
        mcci_port = (MCCIPort) MCCIConnect (server_address, port, NULL, NULL );
        if( ! mcci_port )
          XtscHelpError ("Couldn't make CCI connection" );

        XtFree( server_address ); /* malloc'd in XtscGetServerAddress */

        return( mcci_port );
      }
```

First the routine determines the CCI port number by calling `XtscGetPort()`. Next the browser is started by calling `XtscMosaicStart()` with the port number as its argument. Then, `MCCIInitialize()` does some setup internal to the CCI library. Finally, through a call to `MCCIConnect()`, the CCI channel is established. The return value, `mcci_port`, is a structure that the other CCI functions need to refer to the connection.

The `XtscMosaicGetPort()` function simply returns the value defined by `XTSC_MOSAIC_PORT`. It serves as a building block for a more complicated method of choosing the CCI port:

```
static int XtscMosaicGetPort()
{
    return (XTSC_MOSAIC_PORT );
}
```

To establish the CCI connection, the client must know the machine on which Mosaic is running. The `XtscGetServerAddress()` function finds the name by calling `gethostname()` which, in turn, returns the name of the machine:

```
static char *XtscGetServerAddress( void )
{
    int len;
    char *server_address;
    char hostname[128];

    gethostname (hostname, 128);
    len = strlen(hostname);
    server_address = (char *) XtMalloc ( len +1 );
    strcpy (server_address, hostname);

    return (server_address);
}
```

The `XtscMosaicURL()` function actually requests a URL. Again, this routine is called by `XtscHelpCallback()`. The implementation is shown below:

```
static void XtscMosaicURL( const char *full_url )
{
    int status;

    status = MCCINBGet (mosaic_port, full_url, MCCI_DEFAULT, MCCI_ABSOLUTE,
                        NULL);

    if (status == MCCI_FAIL)
        XtscHelpError ("MCCINBGet failed" );
}
```

`mosaic_port` is a structure that defines the CCI connection. It is assigned in the `XtscMosaicInitialize()` function that is called before `XtscMosaicURL()`.

FUTURE DIRECTIONS

This paper does not cover all possible aspects of the remote control issue. In fact, I wrote the toolkit to serve as a basic building block for more complicated work. Some features that can be improved include:

- The system call in `XtscNetscapeURL()` should be modified to be non-blocking.
- The `XTSC_` definitions should be parameterized, perhaps through resource converters.
- More detailed error handling should be added.

Lastly, the Netscape and Mosaic remote control APIs are new and experimental. They are evolving as rapidly as the rest of the technology surrounding the Internet and will likely change in the near future. If the past is any indication, these changes will be for the better.

REFERENCES

[NCSA95] National Center for Supercomputing Applications. "NCSA Mosaic Common Client Interface." 1995. Available on the World Wide Web at *http://www.ncsa.uiuc.edu/SDG/Software/XMosaic/CCI/cci-spec.html*.

[NCSA95] National Center for Supercomputing Applications. "Application Programmer's Interface for the NCSA Mosaic Common Client Interface (CCI)." 1995. Available on the World Wide Web at *http://www.ncsa.uiuc.edu/SDG/Software/XMosaic/CCI/cci-api.html*.

[Shneiderman92] Shneiderman, Ben. *Designing the User Interface.* Addison-Wesley. 1992.

[Thompson95] Thompson, Dave. "WWW '95 CCI Tutorial." 1995. Available on the World-Wide Web at *http://yahoo.ncsa.uiuc.edu/mosaic/www95talk*.

[Zawinski95] Zawinski, Jamie. "Remote Control of UNIX Netscape." 1995. Available on the World Wide Web at *http://home.netscape.com/newsref/std/x-remote.html* .

GoldenGate: Automatic Conversion and the MediaWarehouse

Douglas S. Rand

Abstract

The GoldenGate and MediaWarehouse projects are part of an overall strategy to facilitate the use of digital media on Silicon Graphics platforms. These projects address the important issues of moving data between different software packages and providing long-term storage for digital media files. This paper discusses the technical challenges of providing these systems.

Doug Rand is a member of SGI's UI Technology Group. Doug is a resident Motif guru having come to SGI after stays at the X Consortium and the Open Software Foundation. He holds a B.S. and an M.S. in electrical engineering from Rensselaer Polytechnic Institute and Dartmouth College, respectively. He can be reached at drand@sgi.com. As usual, much of the credit for this project belongs to people other than the author of the paper: Mike Chow, Dave Curley, and Ken Lee, to name just a few.

INTRODUCTION

GoldenGate provides a standard set of APIs and applications, as well as some automatic support, to enable an application to deal with foreign data formats transparently. The Indigo Magic MediaWarehouse provides digital media data storage for persistent and transient media objects, contains an extensible list of viewers for the different media types, and provides a simple keyword facility for searching the database. In this paper, we'll discuss what GoldenGate and the MediaWarehouse do and how their functionalities are evolving. GoldenGate is known in the actual release as DataConvert, but I'll refer to it here by the development project's name.[†]

As this article goes to press, GoldenGate has matured. In addition to the functionality described here, there are user interface pieces to control the parameters for conversion and a **Save As**... panel for application integration. Over a hundred converters are in the registry for a variety of media formats. The functionality of GoldenGate will be in use in pilot applications as well as being integrated in our version of the Xt Intrinsics library. The MediaWarehouse continues to be refined.

To set the proper tone, imagine that you are an application developer working with digital media. Images, movies, audio and 3D models surround your application, waiting to be used. Intent on providing the best possible application, you spend an enormous amount of time making your application read every possible data format, you release your product and then reality sets in. You find that there are more, newer, maybe even better formats out, and your application can't use them because the support is entirely compiled within the application.

Or, perhaps, you're a game developer. You have thousands of pieces of artwork and audio to integrate into a game. Numerous directories are bulging with your data files with easy-to-understand names like *N000451.gif* and *A0123.au*. In addition to the thousands of hours spent developing the media for the game, you've spent hundreds of hours finding the right selections of media in the file system.

CONVERSION FRAMEWORK

The primary functionality of GoldenGate is the conversion framework. The framework provides a registry of converters and a set of APIs to access the converters to solve problems. A set of panels will be packaged with it, simplifying the process of soliciting user input, when needed, for controlling the conversion process.

MEDIA TYPES AND WHY WE NEED CONVERTERS

One of the areas in greatest need of additional support in X is multimedia. Traditionally, UNIX has been a text-oriented world, and objects representing movies, audio, and images

---

† "DataConvert" somehow loses the meaningful connotations of connectivity and bridging that "GoldenGate" conveys.

haven't received much attention. The ICCCM [Scheifler92], the handbook for describing data exchange and client communication under X, carefully specifies a number of targets for textual data, but only recently has contained any targets for graphical data. A better term for describing an ICCCM target for the uninitiated would be a format. Without standardized formats for exchanging such data, application writers are often unable to exchange data between applications.

For many activities, such as working on audio, developing games, editing video, and authoring CD-ROMs, we need to be able to describe the media and exchange it between applications. In addition to media data, 3D models are becoming increasingly important, and moving the 3D information between applications, such as modelers and renderers, is as frustrating as it is with media data. Since there are a number of 3D formats and no single format is best, there is no common currency nor is there a specific all-inclusive format. The lack of common currency is a real problem with 3D: some formats do a good job of representing geometry, others contain information about material characteristics, and others add information about animation.

Since the different applications may not agree on the format of the data files, we need a framework to translate the data. While such a framework can be external (for example, NetPBM), it is far more convenient to integrate the framework into the application and the underlying libraries.

Since there is no one perfect format exists, one could ask, why not have each program support a canonical format instead of building a conversion framework? The answer is that each format has specific advantages and disadvantages. Using image formats as an example, JPEG[†] provides compact data that has minimal visual artifacts for a maximum of compression. JPEG thus is very good for saving transmission time when moving images and for saving disk space when storing them. But since JPEG is a lossy compression method, drawings with a lot of information in high-frequency components, such as line drawings, are poor candidates for JPEG compression. On the other hand, image formats such as FITS can store virtually everything but create a lot of overhead and large images to move and store, even if the extra information is meaningless to your application. No one format is appropriate for every application.

ICCCM NOMENCLATURE

A brief description of several terms used in this paper can help a reader unfamiliar with the ICCCM. A target in the ICCCM is a *name* (an X atom) that describes a particular kind of data wanted from a selection owner. A *selection owner* is a window that owns the selected data being requested. The *selection* is an atom that is usually one of PRIMARY, CLIPBOARD, or _MOTIF_DROP and is used for primary transfer (usually clicking the middle mouse button), clipboard transfer, or drag and drop, respectively. The data supplied to the requestor has a type, which describes the format of the data (for example,

---

† To be perfectly accurate, JPEG contains a lossless compression format as part of the suite, but most people referring to JPEG are speaking of the lossy compression format.

STRING, INTEGER, etc.), and a format, whose sole purpose is to enable the X server to do the correct byte and word swapping to preserve the data between dissimilar machines.

DIGITAL MEDIA PARAMETERS

While targets and types describe the overall format of a piece of digital media, typing is not sufficient for a complete description. Any particular class of media can have parameters defined to describe the contained data. At this point, GoldenGate defines parameters for images, video, and audio media.

The parameters have two uses. One is descriptive, so that a data receiver can know information about the data received. This is particularly necessary for file formats that do not give all the information themselves—for example, a scale factor for an image file. The second use for the parameters is prescriptive and embodies the use of parameters to control the conversion process itself—for example, asking that the image be converted from RGB to gray scale.

Let's use images again as an example. Digital media parameters let us describe quite a few important characteristics of an image. A partial list for a QuickTime movie might be:

- Size
  DM_IMAGE_HEIGHT = 480
  DM_IMAGE_WIDTH = 640

- Compression mechanism and quality in use
  DM_IMAGE_QUALITY_SPATIAL = .8
  DM_IMAGE_QUALITY_TEMPORAL = .3
  DM_IMAGE_COMPRESSION = "Apple Compact Video"

- Interlacing
  DM_IMAGE_INTERLACING = DM_IMAGE_NONINTERLACED

As you can see, the parameters serve to describe the contents of a particular piece of media. We also have parameters for converters that describe the conversion process.

SCENARIOS

The conversion framework will be used by application developers writing applications that are used with digital media.

The automatic conversion framework is both a standalone API as well as a layer used in conjunction with the X Toolkit Intrinsics to provide conversion to applications utilizing primary transfer, cut and paste, and drag and drop. As shown in Figure 1, a converter in the framework can take input from either a file or a data stream and can provide output to either a file or data stream.

Let's consider some scenarios and how the conversion framework fits into them.

IMAGE PROCESSING

Suppose you work in an image processing lab. Images arrive from a number of sources and in several different formats. These formats include both common ones, such as GIF and JFIF (the file format for JPEG), less common formats (such as FITS), and even a special format peculiar to one of your friends—let's call that PIF (Phil's image file). Before processing it and placing it in an online database of images, you need to convert each file to TIFF and then open the file with your site's application, which allows you to add annotations for the database. The site's application understands TIFF and nothing else.

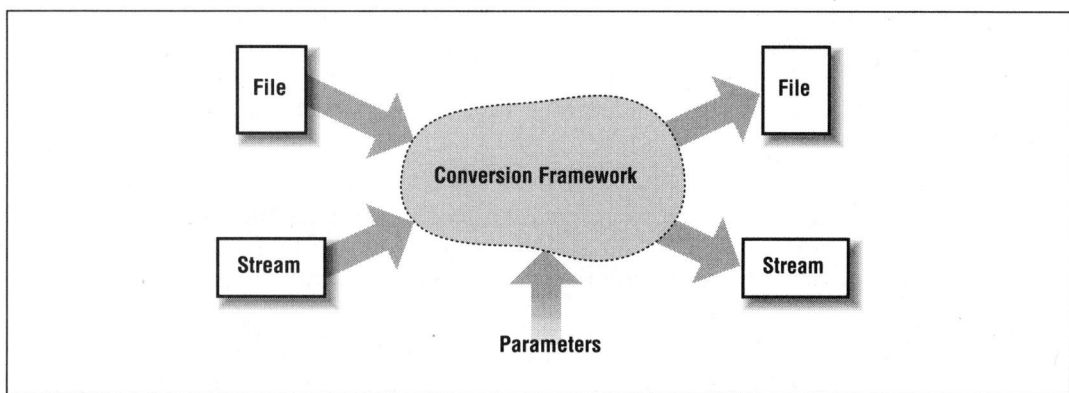

FIGURE 1: *AUTOMATIC CONVERSION ARCHITECTURE*

Each file thus requires that you open a conversion application, convert the file, change to the database application, and read in the file. How can GoldenGate simplify this process?

With GoldenGate, the site's application calls an API that allows the application to ask some questions, most importantly, "What file formats can I convert to TIFF?" Using this information, the file import dialog, another component that GoldenGate will supply, can show file types in addition to TIFF. For example, given the file formats that you receive at the image processing lab, the type menu would show GIF, JFIF, PIF and FITS, in addition to TIFF, if GoldenGate has converters for all these different file types.

When you select a file with one of the file types that are not native to the site's application, the import panel causes a converter to be started to convert the imported file into TIFF format. When this process is finished, the application imports the file. Note, however, that since you no longer have to exit the application, less time is required.

MOVIE MAKING

In this example, you work as a video editor at a local TV station. While most of the station's data is in SGI movie format as a result of the capture program, your favorite editor wants to read in Avid's OMFI. Further, while the editor can output OMFI, the program that does final processing on the resulting video program wants SGI movie. You have to convert each file by running a utility on it, then switch contexts into your editor, take the output of the editor back into the conversion utility, and finally run the post-production program, which takes the output movie file and commits it back to tape.

Using GoldenGate, you open your video editing program and immediately import movies in SGI movie format. Because of GoldenGate, the program receives the movies as OMFI files and reads them in. You edit the footage for the show and write out the result, directly into SGI movie format because GoldenGate translates the output OMFI file into an SGI movie file.

You can now do things that were impossible before. You can run two applications, one of which allows you to call up sequences from a library and view them, and the second of which is your editor. The fetch application allows you to select a sequence based on a time line and thumbnail frames. You then cut that into your editor. Because GoldenGate allows translation of data as part of cut and paste, or drag and drop, the editor receives the data in an understood format.

These scenarios represent the kinds of activities that GoldenGate makes easier. Other examples include working on audio programs, 3D modeling, game development, and authoring CD-ROMs. More prosaic areas benefit as well because GoldenGate allows conversion from one spreadsheet format to another or from WordPerfect to Word.

Once the user has this facility, how is it used? One answer lies within application programs, which are free to call the API to perform conversion where they wish. Users will most commonly use this facility during a save or when exporting data, during an open or when importing data, and during selection transfer. To this end, we intend to provide panels to help the application programmer provide conversion support to the user under these circumstances.

IMPORTING DATA

When the user chooses **Open** or **Import** from the **File** menu, the application can use the GoldenGate import panel, which extends the number of files that the application can load. The application provides a list of understood file types, and then the panel calls the GoldenGate API to extend this list to the other potential types. Our modified version of the file selection dialog can filter the files by type, and thus the import panel displays all the possible file formats that can be opened or imported.

EXPORTING DATA

When the user chooses **Export** or **Save As** from the **File** menu, a similar process occurs, and the user is presented with a list of potential output formats in addition to the ones that the application normally supports. The panel also allows the user to set the digital media parameters on the output file. The parameters are either given to the converter or given directly to the application, depending on whether a converter must be run.

TRANSFERRING DATA

Although transfer does not normally require user intervention, the application can, at the discretion of the application developer, present options to the user during selection transfer. These options allow the user to control parameters for the conversion process, for example, controlling the output sample rate for an audio conversion. A prototype of a panel that controls a conversion process is shown in Figure 2.

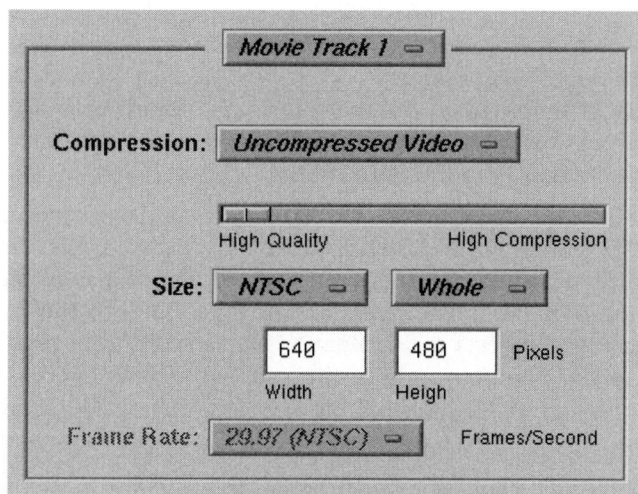

FIGURE 2: *PARAMETER PANEL*

IMPLEMENTATION OF CONVERSION FRAMEWORK

The conversion framework itself consists of two basic parts. One is the mechanism for loading and searching the registry. Another is the actual converter framework that manages the invocation of converters and the movement of data or the creation of files. Both parts are contained in a single dynamic shared object (DSO, essentially a shared library). The converters themselves are also contained in DSOs.

The converters implement a single standard entry point. The actual calling sequence of the converter is slightly different depending on whether the converter is a file or a data stream converter. One or more converters can be contained in each DSO. GoldenGate uses dlopen to open the converter's DSO and dlsym to find the entry point specified in the registry. After that, GoldenGate can call the library function either to evaluate a possible conversion or to perform a conversion.

QUERYING THE REGISTRY

Although the search engine presents an API that allows the programmer to search for converters using arbitrary criteria, it is expected that most queries will be on the from and to type fields. The following fields are in the registry:

- From type

- To type

- Plain language name for converter

- Version

- Description

- Name of DSO

- Entry point name

- Parameter description

Currently the registry is simply an ASCII file, but in the future we may use some form of binary database. Still, current measurements indicate that even with more than 500 entries, the registry is quickly loaded from the ASCII file.

Once a list of converters is returned from a query, the next proper step is to evaluate each converter with the specific input and output parameters desired. Each evaluation presents the parameters to the converter, and the converter can either accept the request or reject it. To do this, the programmer calls an evaluation function with the parameters, and the converter either accepts or rejects the evaluation. Reasonably, the program will probably accept the first converter that responds to the evaluation with success. If the evaluation fails for all converters, it is up to the program whether to retry the evaluation with a less restrictive set of parameters (or no parameters) to attempt to find a converter.

An important feature of the framework is that each converter can be either an entry point in a DSO or a pipeline built out of a set of converters that are connected to form the complete conversion. In the latter case, the evaluation actually evaluates each converter in turn, and only if all the converters accept the conversion is the evaluation successful. The pipelines are a way for users to combine existing converters into custom conversions, which do more complex things to the data. For example, the user could set up a pipeline that scales and then filters an image. Thus, the converters do not all have to actually convert formats; some may simply manipulate data.

If we go back to some of our scenarios, you could imagine that this ability to define new converters from existing ones could be quite handy. In fact, one of the potential future plans for GoldenGate provides a GUI interface to the user to produce custom converters by assembling pipelines.

CONVERTING DATA

Once a converter is chosen, a setup process is performed, which places the convert or set of converters from the pipeline into separate shared memory processes using the `sproc` mechanism. This is similar to a thread but has the added bonus that if the converter raises an exception, the parent process is not terminated. Another view is that `sproc` is like the `fork` system call with shared memory.

Depending on the converter information in the registry, converters get their information either via an API that requires the movement of data along pipes, or they are given input and output filenames to use during conversion.

Each converter obtains data, performs its conversion, and sends the resulting data to the next converter or the process that started the conversion. When the conversion is complete, an end of stream is sent, which terminates the pipes as the data "flows" through the pipeline. Finally the pipeline is destroyed.

Interestingly, when this project was first started, we imagined that using streams to convert data was the most ideal way to perform the task. Architecturally, it had a significant attraction in that the converters didn't need to hold all the data from the entire conversion at all times and that some data would start getting delivered before all the data was supplied. At this point in the project, all the converters are actually file-to-file converters, and the inclusion of the data stream model is being questioned.

For many media formats, the converter needs a file and needs to read from different sections of the file while converting. In fact, since many of the files are mini-databases, such as Apple QuickTime or SGI's Inventor, streaming converters are not possible. For others, in particular the movie formats, the amount of data makes streaming conversion impractical.

EXTENSIONS TO XT AND MOTIF

One of our main goals in providing the data conversion support was to make it as automatic as possible for clients that already support ICCCM [Scheifler92] selection transfer via OSF/Motif and the X Toolkit Intrinsics. Additionally it was felt that future clients should have as much automatic support for conversion of media types as possible.

To this end, the underlying mechanisms in SGI's version of the Xt Intrinsics were changed to use GoldenGate to convert data when the client-supplied convert procedure fails. In addition, the mechanism in our version of Motif for drag and drop was changed to use the GoldenGate API to obtain and extended the target list from the `XmNexportTargets` supplied to the `XmDragContext` [OSF/Motif].

It is worth noting that the Intrinsics support has two variants. For non-incremental transfer, the converted data is passed through the conversion pipeline in a fashion that blocks. The result of the conversion is then returned to the requestor in the usual fashion. For incremental transfer, a work procedure is used to avoid blocking while the converted data is passed through the pipeline. As the requestor's incremental requests are processed, data is read from the pipeline's output and returned.

ICCCM CHANGES PROPOSED

There are two main avenues of extensions being proposed for the ICCCM [Scheifler92]. One extends the standard targets that identify the different data formats agreed upon by the members of the X Consortium. It is too early as this paper is being completed to predict which of these changes will be accepted by the consortium or what form those changes will take. Another avenue would be to add the digital media parameters as a means of modifying a selection request.

As was mentioned earlier, the issue with targets is primarily one of allowing a variety of application writers to exchange data, and not simply for GoldenGate, but also direct exchange of data. Like any language, if the speakers aren't all speaking the same dialect, meaningful communication won't occur.

The use of digital media parameters for modifying a selection request is a logical conclusion of work in the R6 Intrinsics to allow parameterized requests. While it is somewhat more complex to explain this in the multimedia domain, that is the problem area the digital media parameters address.

As you've seen in the earlier section, these parameters allow description of media, and it is not farfetched to extend the notion to controlling media. Targets, such as JPEG_FILE or GIF_FILE, describe the format of the data requested, but they do not talk about the contents of the file. As a concrete example, I might want the data to be transmitted in a lossless or nearly lossless fashion, so I would set the DM_IMAGE_SPATIAL_QUALITY to 1.0. The information is beyond what the target describes but is at least desirable for some applications.

MEDIA WAREHOUSE

The Indigo Magic MediaWarehouse is a facility for storing and retrieving pieces of digital media. In particular, it offers an extensible system of viewers for examining media fragments and the ability to organize the media fragments into larger groups called shelves, which offer permanent storage. The user can search the database via an API and, in addition, can extend the search engine.

The database as supplied is searchable via a keyword search mechanism. Keywords are attached to specific scraps, and the search mechanism allows the retrieval of these. This simple mechanism is really quite powerful because one can, for example, label each image with the location it was taken, such as the city and country name, and then recover all the photos taken in Paris or New York by performing a simple keyword search.

In one sense the MediaWarehouse is an extension of the X clipboard into a general scrapbook that allows the user to view scraps of data, make scraps available for selection transfer, and copy scraps from applications using the X selection transfer mechanism.

DEFINING VIEWERS

Each type of object that can be held in the warehouse can have a defined viewer. The viewers are added by means of an external table, which enables an end user to add new object types without requiring a new release of the warehouse. A section of the current registry file used with the MediaWarehouse is shown below. As you can see, the format is fairly simple to use:

```
! MediaWarehouse configuration file
!
! format is:
!     type_name.viewer: DSO_name
!     type_name.copyFile: True or False
!     type_name.dataAsFile: True or False
!     type_name.iconPanelType: FTR icon type

! misc. text formats
STRING.viewer: /usr/lib/mediaw/libTextViewer.so
STRING.iconPanelType: AsciiTextFile
TEXT.viewer: /usr/lib/mediaw/libTextViewer.so
TEXT.iconPanelType: AsciiTextFile
COMPOUND_TEXT.viewer: /usr/lib/mediaw/libTextViewer.so
COMPOUND_TEXT.iconPanelType: AsciiTextFile

! Inventor 3D format
INVENTOR.viewer: /usr/lib/mediaw/libInventorViewer.so
INVENTOR.copyFile: False
INVENTOR.iconPanelType: InventorBinaryData
```

To add a new viewer, an entry is added with a specified viewer DSO which needs four functions: create, destroy, view and hide. Here's an example from another project which added a viewer:

```
! HTML streams and files
HTML.viewer: /usr/lib/mediaw/libHTMLmediaw.so
HTML.iconPanelType: HTMLDocument
HTML_FILE.viewer: /usr/lib/mediaw/libHTMLmediaw.so
HTML_FILE.iconPanelType: HTMLDocument
HTML_FILE.copyFile: True

! Web Jumper Icons
WebJumpsite.targetType: WEBJUMPER_FILE
WEBJUMPER_FILE.iconPanelType: WebJumpsite
WEBJUMPER_FILE.copyFile: True
WEBJUMPER_FILE.viewer: /usr/lib/mediaw/libHTMLmediaw.so
```

The viewer is in a library *libHTMLmediaw.so,* which defines four entry points. This is referenced in the .viewer resource for each type. Three types are shown here HTML, HTML_FILE, and WEBJUMPER_FILE. These types are used for X selection transfer.

It is also possible to map a media type to a type in the desktop type space where appropriate. The desktop uses file typing rules (FTR) to handle desktop types. The mapping from a media type to a desktop type is handled by the .iconPanelType resource. There are also mappings from desktop types to media types, but these are mostly specified in the actual FTR database. Omissions can be registered here using the `.targetType` resource.

The viewers are being used for more than the MediaWarehouse. SGI's version of the Motif FileSelectionBox can also display a viewer to show the contents of a selected file.

USER MODEL AND APPEARANCE

The user is allowed to move items to and from the warehouse by means of cut and paste, drag and drop, or primary transfer. The resulting object appears in the lower pane show in Figure 3.

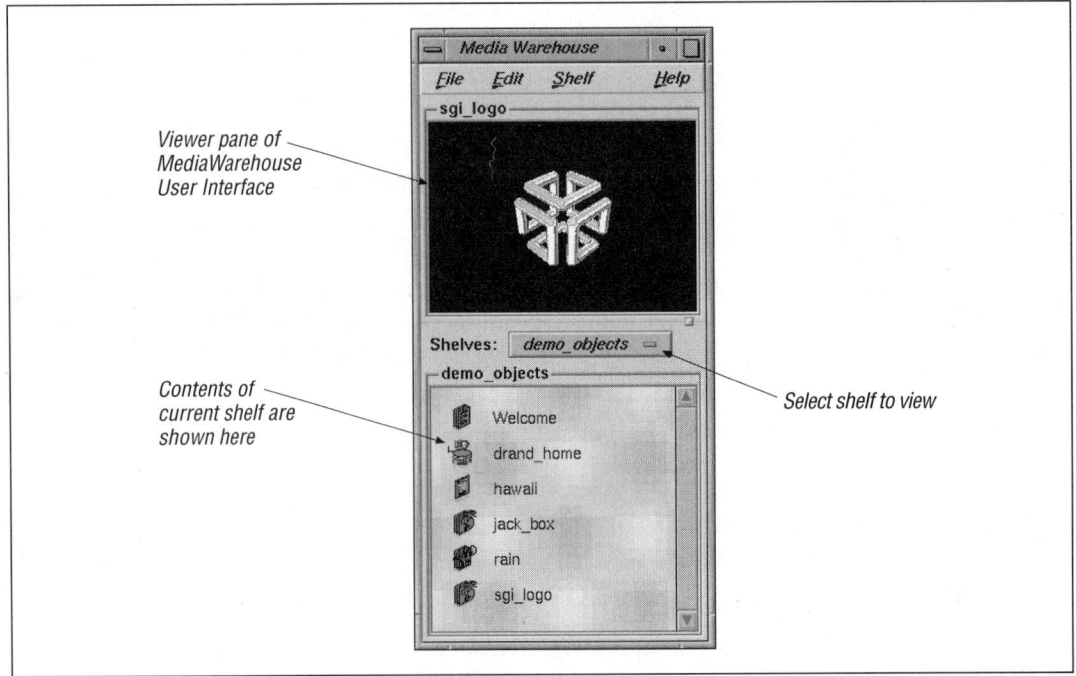

FIGURE 3: *MEDIAWAREHOUSE USER INTERFACE*

The user interface shown in the figure is the current interface, which may be altered before MediaWarehouse ships.

To add an item to a shelf, the user can simply drag and drop it into the contents area. The usual modifier keys for Motif work, including the link operation, which has real meaning to the warehouse. You can also move data to the warehouse using primary transfer or clipboard transfer via the menus. Items can be dragged from the contents area to the desktop or into an application, or they can be selected and transferred using the primary selection via the menus.

Any item in the warehouse may be viewed by selecting it. If there is no registered viewer, the warehouse displays content information in the viewer window.

INTEGRATION WITH GOLDENGATE

At this time, the warehouse stores data in the formats it receives through selection transfer. The warehouse is also integrated with the conversion framework. This significantly adds to the utility of the warehouse by allowing stored data pieces to be pasted in the destination's choice of format, as well as allowing the warehouse to preferentially request data in formats that the user can view.

Let's illustrate with an example. Suppose you spent some time browsing for images for a Web page and placing the interesting images in MediaWarehouse. When you start authoring your page, you use drag and drop to move the images into SGI's Web authoring application. The original image and thus the stored image in the warehouse are in SGI rgb format, but the authoring application wants GIF. GoldenGate handles the conversion automatically when the selection transfer occurs.

FUTURE PLANS

GOLDENGATE

The shape of GoldenGate in the initial release is fairly well set. As the functionality is heading toward a final freeze, we have over a hundred supplied converters for all kinds of media. In addition to the integration into Motif and Xt, there is a command line interface as well.

The future is not clear, but two directions are possible. The current architecture supports a single data stream model, whether that data stream is via a file or via pipes. A dataflow architecture might be an interesting extension. Such an architecture could make it easy to take a set of images and audio data and create a movie.

Another direction that would be exciting is to give the user the ability to create custom converters, even personal converters, via a GUI interface. The GUI interface could allow the user to create a pipeline, set conversion parameters, and try the conversion, looking at the result using the viewer from the MediaWarehouse. When the converter is finished, the user could drag and drop the converter onto the desktop, where she could then drop a file or files directly onto the converter for batch processing.

MEDIAWAREHOUSE

The MediaWarehouse will continue to evolve, and more viewers will be included with it as it ships. The current user interface is expected to evolve as well. In addition, the tight integration with the desktop (for example, drag and drop from the desktop to and from the warehouse) and extensibility of the viewers could lead to novel uses, such as a front end for multimedia databases, or even for those with more specialized information, such as custom molecular design. Multi-user networked and distributed databases using real query languages, such as SQL, could be connected to the warehouse, vastly extending the ability of the MediaWarehouse to act as a query front end for media repositories.

The need for a repository is acute when constructing Web pages. Clearly the warehouse will be used extensively as a repository for clip art. Creating Web pages is a major exercise in searching for and converting media. This will only become more exciting as the Web includes other media types, such as VRML, audio, and movies.

More sophisticated viewers can be implemented. While the viewers are currently output-oriented, future viewers could be made more interactive. For example, a pallet of textures for use with Inventor or other 3D formats could be associated with a viewer, allowing the user to drag and drop a particular texture onto an object.

Last, the MediaWarehouse can evolve to change the way users share data. It can become the core mechanism for both copying objects between users and for linking to networked databases. From there, the warehouse can become more of a groupware tool for sharing all types of media.

REFERENCES

[Scheifler92] Scheifler, R., and J. Gettys. *X Window System*. Digital Press, 1992.

[OSF/Motif] *OSF/Motif Programmer's Reference*. Release 1.2. Prentice Hall.

VISUALIZING X WINDOW SYSTEM PERFORMANCE

Walter D. Lazear

ABSTRACT

Using an X application over the Internet can be a frustrating experience because of the myriad of forces at work that introduce instability. In order to look at the performance problems of a specific application, I devised a method of displaying the network traffic of an X-based application. The technique highlights client and server network interactions, so that patterns of behavior emerge. The resulting display allowed me to spot programming practices that are inappropriate for use on the Internet. This article offers insight into network behavior and encourages further exploration of the visualization technique.

Walt Lazear has been hanging around networks and UNIX systems for over 20 years, first for the U.S. Air Force and then for MITRE Corporation. From the early ARPANET to the latest Internet firewalls, his interests have been technical integrity and improved performance. As a systems engineer, he seeks consistency of design, understanding of processes, and achievable results. As a sailor, he enjoys gunkholing with his wife on the Chesapeake Bay and their backdoor lake.

INTRODUCTION

Using an X application over a wide area network (WAN) like the Internet can be a frustrating experience for a user. Response times can be long, performance can vary, and programs that ran well on local area networks (LANs) can suddenly be unusable. The "biorhythms" of link and router traffic on the Internet can conspire to create congestion points that play havoc with performance. The congestion points can vaporize and reform elsewhere in response to bursts of traffic on the Internet. One thing the Internet guarantees is variability when you have to traverse five or six network administrations.

A military customer had developed a set of applications to be launched by a commercial X-based desktop. The customer wanted people at other military sites to be able to use these applications; running them over the Internet seemed like a natural way to accomplish this. Others could log into the first site, run the applications, and display them on their own workstations. Although performance was acceptable on the customer's LAN, the applications required over 20 minutes to start over the Internet. Measurements taken of the network showed that the data packets were being forwarded through 22 to 24 routers along the way. They also showed that the round-trip times were approximately a half second and that up to 15% of the packets were lost due to congestion on the Internet. While of serious concern, these performance characteristics did not account for why displaying the first window required a half hour. I was asked to diagnose this problem.

I'll admit up front that X programming is a weak aspect of my skill set, so I needed a quick way to get on top of the application without having access to source code. To apply my knowledge of data communications protocols and network infrastructure, I needed to gain a feeling for what these applications were doing to the network. I used a protocol analyzer to capture a detailed interpretation of each packet sent between the client application and the display server. The first 20 interpreted packets of an *xterm* process starting up are shown below:

```
Pkt   Delta  Dst Src  Summary
463   0.3555  S   A   DLC Ethertype=0800, size=60 bytes
                      IP  D=[S] S=[A] LEN=20
                      TCP D=6000 S=1257 SYN
464   0.0008  A   S   DLC Ethertype=0800, size=60 bytes
                      IP  D=[A] S=[S] LEN=20
                      TCP D=1257 S=6000 SYN ACK=1193344001
465   0.0015  S   A   DLC Ethertype=0800, size=60 bytes
                      IP  D=[S] S=[A] LEN=20
                      TCP D=6000 S=1257  ACK=552896001
467   0.0084  S   A   DLC Ethertype=0800, size=66 bytes
                      IP  D=[S] S=[A] LEN=32
                      TCP D=6000 S=1257  ACK=552896001
                      XWIN C Connection Setup MSB V11.0
469   0.0017  A   S   DLC Ethertype=0800, size=326 bytes
                      IP  D=[A] S=[S] LEN=292
```

```
                    TCP  D=1257 S=6000   ACK=1193344013
                    XWIN R Connection Setup Success V11.0.5000 Image=MSB
                          Bitmap=MSB "MIT X Consortium"
471   0.0074  S  A  DLC Ethertype=0800, size=102 bytes
                    IP   D=[S] S=[A] LEN=68
                    TCP  D=6000 S=1257   ACK=552896273
                    XWIN C Create GC Fore=1 Back=0
                    XWIN C Get Property RESOURCE_MANAGER
472   0.0019  A  S  DLC Ethertype=0800, size=450 bytes
                    IP   D=[A] S=[S] LEN=416
                    TCP  D=1257 S=6000   ACK=1193344061
                    XWIN R Get Property STRING "OpenWindows.
                          ScrollbarPlacement:<09>right<0A> OpenWindows.
                          DragRightDistance:<09>100<0A>OpenWindows... ...
474   0.0855  S  A  DLC Ethertype=0800, size=78 bytes
                    IP   D=[S] S=[A] LEN=44
                    TCP  D=6000 S=1257   ACK=552896669
                    XWIN C Intern Atom "SCREEN_RESOURCES"
475   0.0013  A  S  DLC Ethertype=0800, size=86 bytes
                    IP   D=[A] S=[S] LEN=52
                    TCP  D=1257 S=6000   ACK=1193344085
                    XWIN R Intern Atom NONE
479   0.0607  S  A  DLC Ethertype=0800, size=82 bytes
                    IP   D=[S] S=[A] LEN=48
                    TCP  D=6000 S=1257   ACK=552896701
                    XWIN C Intern Atom "WM_CONFIGURE_DENIED"
480   0.0012  A  S  DLC Ethertype=0800, size=86 bytes
                    IP   D=[A] S=[S] LEN=52
                    TCP  D=1257 S=6000   ACK=1193344113
                    XWIN R Intern Atom 175
481   0.0024  S  A  DLC Ethertype=0800, size=70 bytes
                    IP   D=[S] S=[A] LEN=36
                    TCP  D=6000 S=1257   ACK=552896733
                    XWIN C Intern Atom "WM_MOVED"
482   0.0012  A  S  DLC Ethertype=0800, size=86 bytes
                    IP   D=[A] S=[S] LEN=52
                    TCP  D=1257 S=6000   ACK=1193344129
                    XWIN R Intern Atom 176
483   0.0286  S  A  DLC Ethertype=0800, size=60 bytes
                    IP   D=[S] S=[A] LEN=20
                    TCP  D=6000 S=1257   ACK=552896765
491   0.0386  S  A  DLC Ethertype=0800, size=458 bytes
                    IP   D=[S] S=[A] LEN=424
                    TCP  D=6000 S=1257   ACK=552896765
```

```
            XWIN C Open Font "cursor"
            XWIN C (7) Create Glyph Cursors Char=152; Char=116;
               Char=108; Char=114; Char=106; Char=110; Char=112
            XWIN C Create Pixmap Area=2*2
            XWIN C Create GC Fore=1 Back=0
            XWIN C Put Image Format=Bitmap Area=2*2 at 0,0 [8 bytes]
            XWIN C Free GC
            XWIN C Create GC Fore=1 Back=0 Fill=Opaque-stippled
            XWIN C (2 more) Create Glyph Cursor, Query Colors
  496  0.0036  A  S  DLC Ethertype=0800, size=102 bytes
            IP   D=[A] S=[S] LEN=68
            TCP D=1257 S=6000   ACK=1193344533
            XWIN R Query Colors
   . . .
```

As you can see, the output is quite detailed. I could also have used the program *xmon* to capture the necessary detail. Through the use of *sed* and *awk*, the output from either the analyzer or *xmon* could be reduced to a simple list of X Window System commands, replies, and events. This list was too detailed, however, for the overall view that I wanted. I needed a way to simplify the data and be able to get an "X at a glance" view of the application's behavior.

X-AT-A-GLANCE

I decided to create a graphical "signature" of this behavior by summarizing the detail produced by the monitoring program by using visualization. In this way, I hoped not only to learn what the application was doing but to spot behavior patterns that could be adversely influenced by delays introduced by the Internet. My approach was simple: assign each type of X command, reply, and event a number, and plot them chronologically. I used *xgraph* for my plots, but any plotting tool would work. The X-axis on the graph is the order in which the commands or events occurred (just an increasing sequence number). The Y-axis is the assigned number of the command or event.

The numbers I assigned were somewhat arbitrary (see Table 1), but I tried to functionally group related commands, hoping to see close-knit clusters of commands in actual usage. For example, all the commands related to fonts are grouped together because I thought font manipulation might plot as a recognizable shape at a specific level. The goal was to reduce the visual "noise" level and to let patterns emerge.

To clarify the behavior of the application further, I assigned client commands positive numbers, while assigning the corresponding server replies the corresponding negative numbers. Events generated by the server were plotted in a distinct negative range (-7 to -19). Thus, client and server actions would plot in different parts of the overall graph. This would ensure that I could see clearly those items originated by the client and those by the server. By connecting the plotted commands and events with lines, I should be able easily

ITEM TYPE	NR	ITEM TYPE	NR	ITEM TYPE	NR
Send Event	-7	Create GC	90	Destroy Window	181
Reparent Notify	-8	Free GC	91	Configure Window	182
Client Message	-9	Change GC	92	Map Window	183
Configure Notify	-10	Query Extension	93	Map Subwindows	184
Button Press/Rlse	-12	Create Pixmap	100	Query Tree	186
Focus In/Out	-13	Put Image	101	Window Error	187
Enter/Leave Notify	-14	Free Pixmap	102	Change Window	188
Destroy Notify	-15	Create Glyph	103	Alloc Named	200
Map/Unmap Notify	-16	Graphics Exposure	104	Translate Coords	201
(Yes/No) Exposure	-18	Recolor Cursor	110	Intern Atom	202
Motion Notify	-19	Alloc Color	111	Set Close	203
XWIN Reply	0	Lookup Color	112	Get Modifier	204
Connection Setup	2	Query Colors	113	Get Input	205
Create Cursor	50	Get Keyboard	120	Get Selection	206
Query Best	60	Key Press	121	Set Selection	207
Get Geometry	62	Key Release	122	Poly Segment	220
Open Font	70	Property Notify	140	Poly Line	221
Close Font	71	Change Property	141	Copy Area	222
Query Font	72	Delete Property	142	Clear Area	223
List Fonts	73	Get Property	143	Fill Poly	224
Grab Buttons	80	Image Text8	170	Poly Rectangle	225
Grab Server	81	Poly Text8	171	Copy Plane	226
Ungrab Server	82	Poly Point	172	Set Clip	227
Grab Keys	83	Create Window	180		
Ungrab Pointer	84	Unmap Window	185		

TABLE 1: *ASSIGNED VALUES*

to spot client/server interactions that could be delayed by poor Internet performance (such as when the client required a reply before sending the next command).

Figure 1 shows the plot of xterm starting up. The sequence starts with an exchange of Connection Setup (command 2 and reply -2), followed by a Create GC command (90), several Get Property command exchanges (143 and -143), and so on. The resulting plot resembles the seismic signature of an earthquake. Indeed, when the plotted lines cross the zero mark, they indicate delay-sensitive behavior in an application. Long sequences of commands from the client to the server are essentially one-way and are not heavily influenced by delay or congestion in the intervening network. Switching between client- and server-initiated items, however, indicates a half-duplex behavior that is directly influenced by degraded network performance. This situation can render applications useless over the Internet.

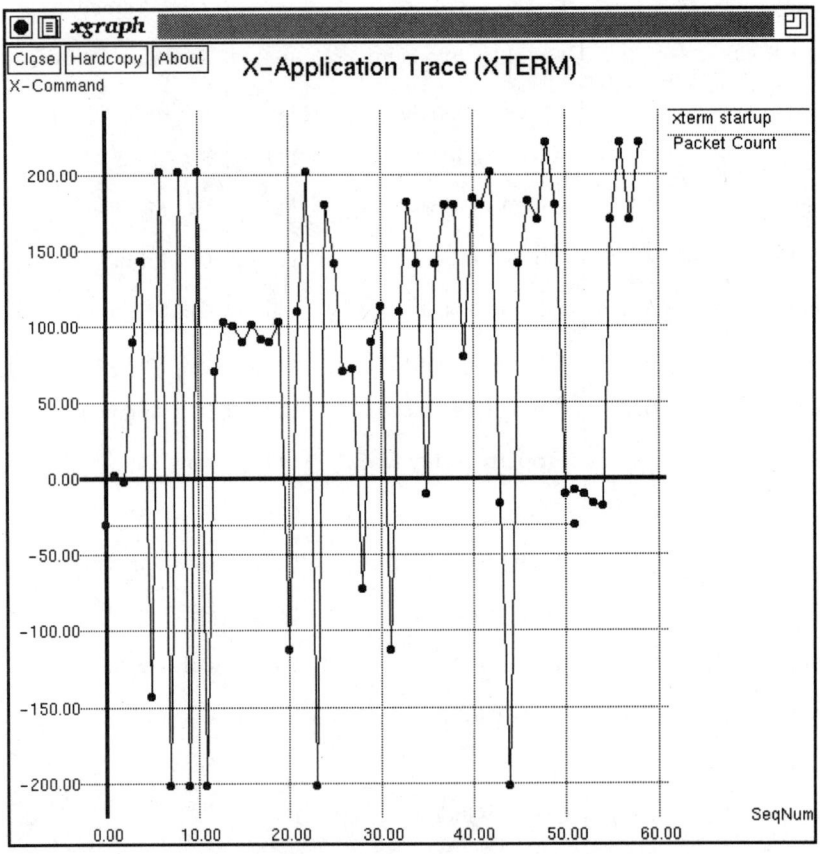

FIGURE 1: *XTERM APPLICATION TRACE*

FALLOUT

One of the early results of plotting applications in this way was that I could spot behavior that can overload a network in ways unintended by the X programmer. Exploration of this phenomenon through discussions with programmers revealed a serious drawback inherent in modern X programming: the use of GUI builders and high-level APIs by programmers isolates them from the network. They assume that network capacity is infinite (or at least adequate) for any style of programming and interaction. Another assumption many programmers make is that the API library routines are efficient in their network usage. Alas, they may not be very gentle on the network at all. Inefficient network usage is not so serious when the library routines are running on a LAN with high bandwidth but can be crucial when they're running over a WAN. The result is that programmers are not aware of what they have imposed on the network and are surprised to see the behavior that my plots record.

SERVER BEHAVIOR

One such behavior is the continuous sending of "cursor motion" events by the server to the client (see packets 85-145 in Figure 2). In this mode, the client typically wants to change the surface shading or border color of objects such as buttons when the cursor moves over the object. To achieve this, the client must know at all times where the pointing device is. While this is an attractive feature of an application's graphical interface, it wreaks havoc across a WAN by clogging the network with a continuous packet stream.

In Figure 2, I have plotted the dialog of a confirmation window presented to the user by a proxy supporting X through a firewall. After painting the window and two buttons, the server starts sending cursor motion events continuously until a button is pressed. The server in this case generated 24 packets per second. The client changed the highlighting (at sequence number 100) when it detected the cursor had moved over a button. The traffic stream of events can help to clog a WAN link and cause performance degradation on other systems. Perhaps it could have been avoided by merely sending a cursor position at the time of the button press and foregoing the visual changes. The feedback of changing the color of the outline of a button seems a minor gain compared to the performance hit the network takes in this case. If designed for a LAN, the application proxy can survive with the present behavior. If intended to run over a WAN, the application proxy should be redesigned.

CLIENT'S TURN

Another example of detected behavior is the constant polling by the client for the user's keyboard input (see Figure 3). This is the opposite direction from the server's sending cursor motion events. Instead of being a one-way torrent, however, this behavior is made up of pairs of packets started by the client. There is a polling command to "get input" from the client and a corresponding reply from the server. The good news is that only one command is outstanding at a time. The bad news is that this ping-pong match

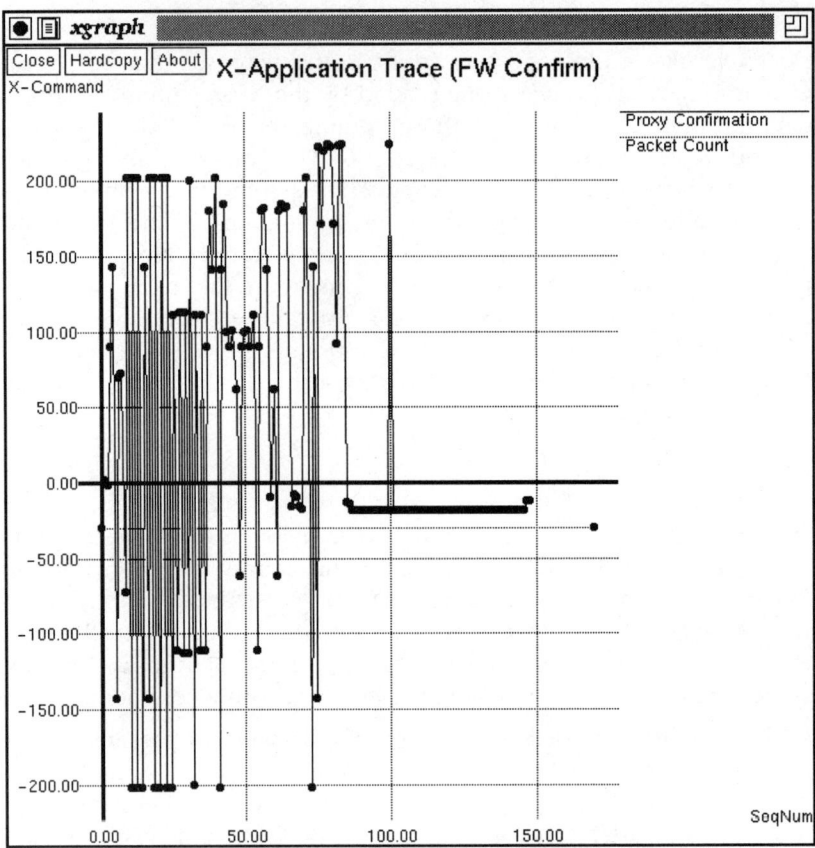

FIGURE 2: *CONFIRMATION WINDOW TRACE*

continues before, during, and after the user types characters and that it puts extra packets on the network.

The application shown in Figure 3 painted a form on the user's screen (packets 500-1560) and then waited for the user to type characters into an area of the form (starting with packet 1594). There was no notion of sleeping until the user started typing, just a brute force polling technique. Figure 4 shows the detail of the start of the command/reply sequence.

BACK TO BASICS

The original performance problem that I was diagnosing was the extremely long startup time of a desktop application launcher. The plot for this program's startup is shown in Figure 5. This program took approximately 3 to 4 minutes to start on a LAN but when run across the Internet, could take up to 30 minutes to display the first window.

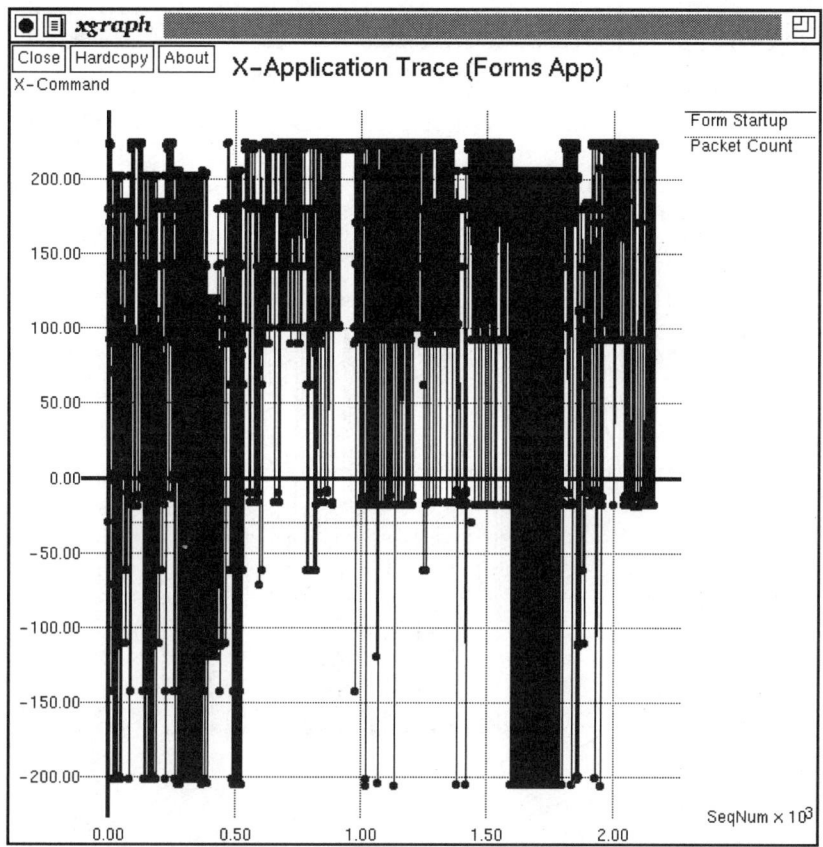

FIGURE 3: *FORMS APPLICATION TRACE*

When I monitored and plotted this application, I discovered that it required many thousands of commands to set up its X environment on the server (sequence numbers 500-4700 in Figure 5). The majority of the commands were in the stop-and-wait or half-duplex mode mentioned earlier. Figure 6 shows the two packet-exchange styles that dominate the startup conversation. This figure is a greatly enlarged view of the center of Figure 5.

Among its other activities during startup, the application sent 2,100 commands for setup and received 2,100 immediate replies from the server. On a LAN, this took 3 to 4 minutes and lots of network activity, but the LAN's bandwidth supported it. On a WAN, the long round-trip times between command and reply meant that the startup required a significantly longer time. Even if no retransmissions were required over the WAN, the delays force a minimum period for this entire exchange, which is equal to 2,300 multiplied by the round-trip time. On a WAN experiencing a quarter-second round-trip time, this results in a minimum startup time of 525 seconds (almost nine minutes). Clearly, eliminating the half-duplex behavior would greatly help the performance of the application. The type of behavior I detected from this application and the unpredictable nature of the Internet

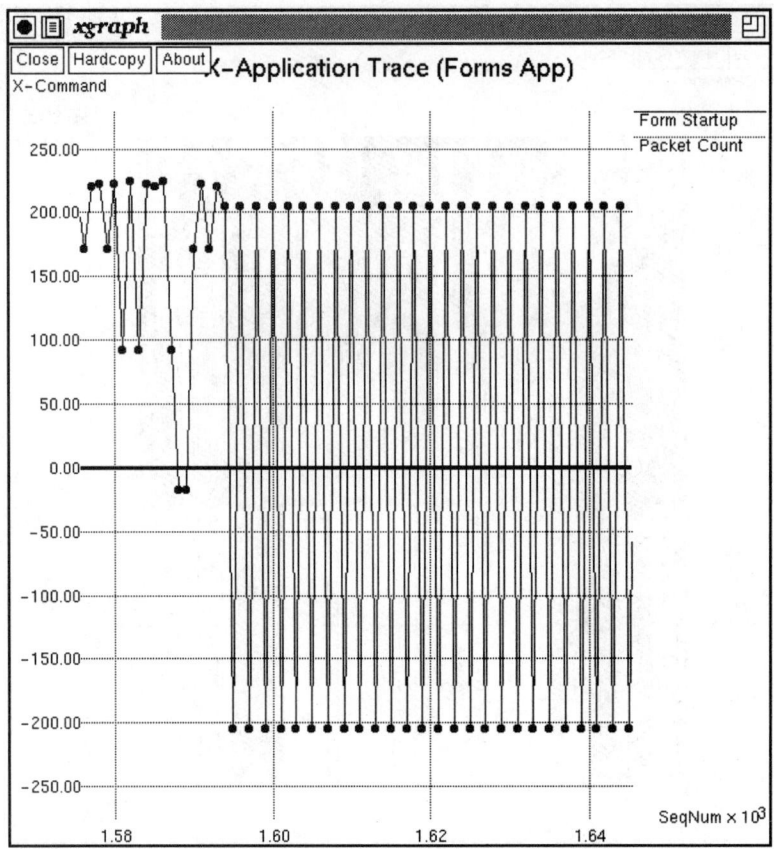

FIGURE 4: *FORMS APPLICATION DETAIL*

conspire to create unhappy users. Because of this investigation, the deployment plan for this application is under review.

ALTER EGOS

To measure another aspect of the performance of the X applications, I counted the number of packets used in the conversation being analyzed. I plotted the number of packets on the visualization graph to easily spot the correspondence and density of requests to packets. Most applications put a single X command in a packet.

I also characterized an application by the ratio of server requests to total requests during a conversation. If the client and server sent the same number of requests, the ratio would be 0.5, which indicates a probable half-duplex behavioral problem. If the ratio is down in the 0.2 range, the server is generating relatively less traffic, and the client dominates the

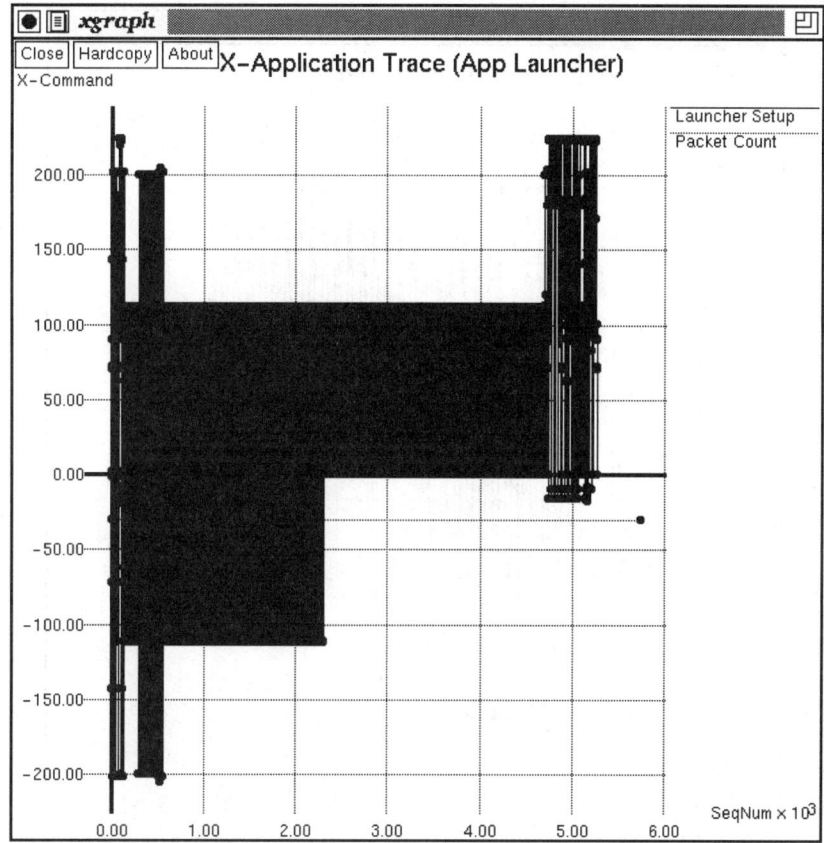

FIGURE 5: *APPLICATION LAUNCHER TRACE*

conversation as one would like. For example, *xterm* has a ratio of 0.30, but the application launcher has a ratio of 0.44 and a real problem with Internet performance.

ISSUES

What else can we determine about X applications from this visualization technique? Groups of commands are probably presented in an inefficient order, causing some commands to be repeated later to undo or redo previous actions. Careful use of my simple visualization technique could spot those sequences. My limited experience with X programming did not allow me to take advantage of this aspect of analysis.

The protocol analyzer I used broke down the TCP payload into individual X commands for most packets. Some packets, however, were summarized in an incomplete description using ellipses (...) to indicate that there were more uninterpreted commands (for an example, see packet 472 in the analyzer output shown earlier). Thus, some of the X

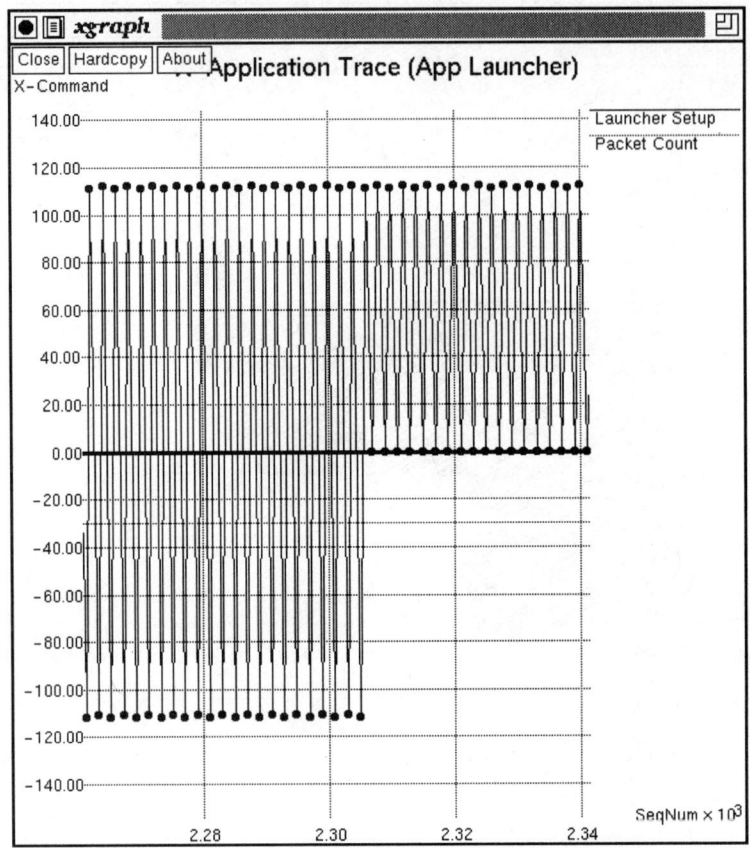

FIGURE 6: *APPLICATION LAUNCHER DETAIL*

commands appear neither in the points files nor in the final plot. Using some other method to capture the X commands (such as **xmon**) could make the results more accurate. It should be noted that the point of visualization is not to focus on detail, however, but to highlight large patterns. Nevertheless, it would be useful to have all commands accounted for.

My investigation concentrated mainly on the startup behavior of the various applications. Further studies could look at the actual interaction with the user over the life of the applications. I have discussed a couple of behaviors, but most certainly others are to be discovered and analyzed.

CONCLUSION

My approach to X application visualization allows a network analyst to detect and focus on behavior potentially detrimental to performance. Programmers can use this technique to see what network traffic their code generates. Applied during development, this technique can identify potential performance problems, which can make an application's performance suitable over a broader networking environment.

Improvements could be made to my visualizations. One could better group the X functions to create more cohesive visual patterns. One could parse the protocol analyzer output to retain more detail when multiple commands are stacked into one packet. One could introduce color to highlight bursts of activity, long repetitions, or highly undesirable behavior.

I have tried to show how I used visualization to understand an application's behavior on a network. I enjoyed the challenge of simplifying my analysis of a network performance problem. I hope this discussion of a simple approach to visualizing X behavior will stimulate others to think about other innovative approaches.

THE PANORAMIX EXTENSION

Madeline T. Asmus

ABSTRACT

It has become commonplace for workstations to support more than one monitor. The use of sophisticated window managers such as *mwm* and *twm* makes displaying many different client applications on multiple screens inexpensive, easy, and intuitive. The ability to use a menu to bring up an *xterm*, size it, type in it, and iconify it is within the reach of all users. However, using a multi-headed display becomes uncomfortable when the user moves a window to the edge of a screen. When a window extends beyond the edge of a screen, parts of the window disappear. When using more than one screen, the user expects the window's motion to continue, with the window appearing on the adjacent screen. Unfortunately, the standard behavior of a multi-headed X environment is not intuitive in this way. The PanoramiX Extension is the Digital solution for a multi-headed environment; it provides the intuitive interface that is lacking in the multi-headed environment.

Madeline T. Asmus is a Digital Equipment Corporation employee working on the Digital UNIX XServer project.

Introduction

The PanoramiX Extension provides a way for a multi-headed system to function as one large screen. Windows can span multiple screens and can move from one screen to another.

Currently, the PanoramiX Extension works in a homogeneous graphics environment. A graphics environment is considered homogeneous if, for example, all of the graphics cards have 8 planes with 6 visuals. Mixing a 24-plane graphics card with a 8-plane card creates a heterogeneous environment. Support for heterogeneous graphics environments is planned for a future releases.

Unlike other multiple screen implementations, such as Xvan [Jones94], PanoramiX provides a solution at the device-independent level. The advantage of this approach is that it reduces the amount of work involved in supporting and maintaining the extension. The number of graphics devices on the market continues to grow; embedding the extension functionality into the device-dependent code for each device would be a maintenance nightmare. Since the PanoramiX implementation does not require any low-level graphics modifications, existing device-dependent code does not have to be recompiled. In the loadable server world, the PanoramiX Extension will work with existing device-dependent shared libraries.

While there are benefits to not integrating the PanoramiX functionality with low-level graphics code, this implementation does require some maintenance at the device-independent level. This paper describes the areas that require maintenance. After providing an overview of the design, the paper describes the implementation of the extension, which is split into two parts: the actual extension code and modifications to the X server code.

Digital has successfully implemented the PanoramiX Extension at the device-independent level for X11R6. The current implementation is being made available to consumers of the Digital UNIX 4.0 release in the form of an Advanced Developers Kit.

Design Overview: The big picture

The PanoramiX Extension makes client applications believe that the workstation is supporting only one screen (screen0); the size of this composite screen is that of the multiple screens combined. The extension makes a client believe that there is only one screen by intercepting X Window System protocol messages when they are dispatched. The extension handles requests by:

- Wrapping GCOps and GCFuncs calls
- Wrapping screen functions in the ScreenPtr
- Calling replacement functions for routines that are not defined by the ProcVector array—for instance, ProcCreateWindow

In each case, for each physical screen, the alternate function calls the original function with a different set of resources and with the coordinates adjusted for the single screen.

For instance, a drawing command received from the client is modified for each screen by adjusting the coordinates to be consistent with the screen's position relative to the internal `screen0`.

It is necessary to create multiple instances of some resources because these resource are screen-unique or they contain a back pointer to a `ScreenPtr`. These resources include GCs, windows, pixmaps, and colormaps. When the server handles a client request that creates a resource, the extension creates an equivalent instance of the resource for each physical screen. PanoramiX uses linked lists to keep track of these resources; each entry in a list contains the following information:

- The client-requested resource identifier
- Additional resource identifiers created by the extension
- A Boolean used for freeing entries

The extension uses a separate linked list for each type of resource: GCs, windows, pixmaps, and colormaps. The extension creates an entry in the appropriate list for each protocol request that creates a resource. The first field in the entry is always the client-requested identifier passed by the client request. The additional resource identifiers are created by using `FakeClientID`. These additional resource identifiers are used for keeping track of the resources created for each physical screen. The Boolean `FreeMe` is used to mark a list entry for deletion.

When a client creates a window, the extension creates a window for each physical screen. Entities drawn in a window are actually drawn into each of the equivalent windows. Since the standard clipping logic draws only those pixels that fall within the range of each screen, the image on the screen looks as it should.

When an event is sent to a client, it is modified to look as if it is coming from a client-known entity. For instance, an `Expose` event for a window on `screen1` is modified so that it appears to the client that it came from a window on `screen0`, since that is the only screen the client knows about.

Resources are deleted for two reasons: an explicit client request to destroy a window or a `CloseDownClient` request. When `CloseDownClient` is called, all of the resources associated with a given client are freed. This means that all the PanoramiX IDs associated with each resource have to be freed. Whenever a resource is freed, the ID is cross-searched in the PanoramiX linked lists by type. If there is a match, the entry is marked so that it can be freed. The actual freeing of marked PanoramiX entries occurs after every invocation of `FreeClientResources`.

PANORAMIX IMPLEMENTATION

The extension is implemented in three files: a header file that defines PanoramiX structures, a C file that handles the extension initialization, and a C file that implements the replacement functions.

HEADER FILE

The file */xc/include/extensions/panoramiX.h* defines the PanoramiX linked list data structures, as well as macros that are used to perform operations on the linked lists. As already described, the extension creates a separate linked list for GCs, windows, colormaps, and pixmaps. A PanoramiX linked list is defined as follows:

```
typedef struct _PanoramiXList {
    struct _PanoramiXList *next;
    Bool FreeMe;
    PanoramiXInfo info[MAXSCREENS];
} PanoramiXList;
```

The `PanoramiXInfo` array stores the resource ID requested by the client, as well as by the additional resource IDs created by the extension.

The extension uses a data structure to keep track of the position of a drawing relative to a physical screen. This data structure is defined as follows:

```
typedef struct _PanoramiXData {
    int above;
    int below;
    int left;
    int right;
    int x;
    int y;
    int width;
    int height;
} PanoramiXData;
```

The `x`, `y`, `width`, and `height` fields are what you would expect. The `above`, `below`, `left`, and `right` fields are used to describe the position of the physical screen relative to the other screens.

The header file defines macros that are used to find, mark, and free entries in the linked lists.

The macros `PANORAMIXFIND_ID`, `PANORAMIXFIND_ID_BY_SCRNUM`, `PANORAMIX-FIND_LAST` are used to search any of the linked lists for a matching ID. `PANORAMIXFIND_ID` searches a linked list for a matching ID indexed by the root window, while `PANORAMIXFIND_ID_BY_SCRNUM` searches for a matching ID indexed by a screen number. `PANORAMIXFIND_LAST` returns the last entry in a linked list.

The macros `FORCE_ROOT` and `FORCE_WIN` are used when the X server sends an event to a client. These macros find a matching ID in the appropriate linked list and return the real window ID value. The macro `SKIP_FAKE_WINDOW` is also used when the X server sends events. If this macro finds a matching ID, it causes the calling routine to return without sending a reply to the client.

The extension uses the **PANORAMIX_MARKFREE** macro when client resources are being freed. This macro searches a PanoramiX linked list based on the resource type of the resource ID. If it finds any matching IDs, the entries are marked for freeing. The **PANORAMIX_FREE** macro is used after client resources have been freed and the PanoramiX linked list entries have been marked with **PANORAMIX_MARKFREE**. **PANORAMIX_FREE** checks all the entries in the linked lists; any entries that have been marked for freeing are removed and freed from the list.

EXTENSION INITIALIZATION

The file */xc/programs/Xserver/Xext/panoramiX.c* contains the PanoramiX extension initialization routine, as well as routines that handle screen consolidation and creating the connection block.

PanoramiXExtensionInit() is called from the standard server extension initialization code. This occurs after **InitOutput** has run, so the number of physical screens and information pertaining to them is available to the extension. The initialization handles the following tasks:

- Makes the PanoramiX Extension available by calling **AddExtension**
- Allocates memory for the **panoramiXdataPtr** structures and the **PanoramiXWin-Root**, **PanoramiXGCRoot**, **PanoramiXCmapRoot**, and **PanoramiXPmapRoot** linked lists
- Positions the screens based on the *-edge* command-line option or in a simple left-to-right sequence
- Wraps certain screen functions and replaces the dispatch functions

PanoramiXConsolidate() function is called from **main()**, after the font path, the default font, and the root cursor have been established. This routine assigns the root window and colormap IDs in the PanoramiX linked lists.

PanoramiXCreateConnectionBlock() is called from **main()** instead of **CreateConnectionBlock**. The PanoramiX routine calls the standard **CreateConnectionBlock** routine and then modifies certain elements of the **ConnectionBlock** structure to represent one screen with the total width and height of the combined screens. This routine is what makes a client believe that the multi-headed system has only one screen.

PANORAMIX REPLACEMENT FUNCTIONS

The file */xc/programs/Xserver/Xext/panoramiXprocs.c* implements the replacement functions used by the extension. In general, functions in this category simply extend on the standard device-independent server functions by performing the following steps, once for each physical screen:

1. Validate the protocol message, same as in base function.
2. Locate the resource (window, GC, pixmap, or colormap) in linked lists.

3. If the protocol operation creates a resource, append that resource to the related PanoramiX linked list.

4. Loop through the `ProcVector` routine once per screen, substituting the screen-unique resource IDs as appropriate.

5. If the `ProcVector` routine doesn't return successfully or if the operation destroys a resource, remove it from the related PanoramiX linked list.

The replacement functions for the PanoramiX extension are listed in Table 1.

PanoramiXCreateWindow()	PanoramiXChangeWindowAttributes()
PanoramiXDestroyWindow()	PanoramiXDestroySubwindows()
PanoramiXChangeSaveSet()	PanoramiXReparentWindow()
PanoramiXMapWindow()	PanoramiXMapSubwindows()
PanoramiXUnmapWindow()	PanoramiXUnmapSubwindows()
PanoramiXConfigureWindow()	PanoramiXCirculateWindow()
PanoramiXGetGeometry()	PanoramiXChangeProperty()
PanoramiXDeleteProperty()	PanoramiXSendEvent()
PanoramiXCreatePixmap()	PanoramiXFreePixmap()
PanoramiXCreateGC()	PanoramiXChangeGC()
PanoramiXCopyGC()	PanoramiXSetDashes()
PanoramiXSetClipRectangle()	PanoramiXFreeGC()
PanoramiXClearToBackground()	PanoramiXCopyArea()
PanoramiXCopyPlane()	PanoramiXPolyPoint()
PanoramiXPolyLine()	PanoramiXPolySegment()
PanoramiXPolyRectangle()	PanoramiXPolyArc()
PanoramiXFillPoly()	PanoramiXPolyFillRectangle()
PanoramiXPolyFillArc()	PanoramiXPutImage()
PanoramiXGetImage()	PanoramiXPolyText()
PanoramiXImageText8()	PanoramiXImageText16()
PanoramiXCreateColormap()	PanoramiXFreeColormap()

TABLE 1: *PANORAMIX REPLACEMENT FUNCTIONS*

PanoramiXInstallColormap()	PanoramiXUninstallColormap()
PanoramiXAllocColor()	PanoramiXAllocNamedColor()
PanoramiXAllocColorCells()	PanoramiXFreeColors()
PanoramiXStoreColors()	

TABLE 1: *PANORAMIX REPLACEMENT FUNCTIONS (CONTINUED)*

SERVER CODE CHANGES

In addition to the actual code for the PanoramiX Extension, various changes to the X server code were required to implement the extension. The file */xc/programs/Xserver/mi/ miinitext.c* was modified to define the `PanoramiXExtensionInit()` routine and */xc/ programs/Xserver/os/utils.c* was changed to recognize the *panoramiX* command-line argument.

In */xc/programs/Xserver/mi/miinitext_load.c*, the code for `InitExtensions` and `LoadQueryExtensions` was modified to check for PanoramiX shared libraries. The check in `InitExtensions` allows the extension to be loaded at server startup, while the second check keeps the server from loading the extension if it is not being used. When the extension is not being used, the `noPanoramiXExtension` flag is set to `True`.

The config file */xc/config/cf/Project.tmpl* defines `PANORAMIX`. This provides a mechanism for describing all PanoramiX code changes in the X server within `ifdef` statements, similar to other X server extensions.

MAIN

In */xc/programs/Xserver/dix/main.c*, a call to `PanoramiXConsolidate()` was added after the font initialization process and prior to the initialization of the root window. The `main()` routine also calls the `PanoramiXCreateConnectionBlock()` routine. This routine also handles cleaning up after the extension when the server is reset. When the server enters into a reset situation, PanoramiX structures are freed so as not to hog memory. Prior to freeing the resources, the current value of `noPanoramiXExtension` is saved, and the flag is set to `True`. This is done because the extension needs to match only real window IDs to mark list entries for freeing. After the resources are freed, `noPanoramiXExtension` is set back to its original saved value.

DISPATCH

Several functions are replaced at the dispatch level, as described in the design overview presented earlier. The `Dispatch()` routine in */xc/programs/Xserver/dix/dispatch.c* was modified to implement the replacement of the functions by calling the alternate PanoramiX functions instead of the original X server functions.

Some of the replacements routines are implemented by saving the original `ProcVector` and replacing selected entries with routines that call the original `ProcVector` routine for each screen. The modified `ProcVector` is restored on X server reset if the PanoramiX Extension exits. The requests included in this category are shown in Table 2.

CreateWindow	ChangeWindowAttributes
DestroyWindow	DestroySubwindows
ChangeSaveSet	ReparentWindow
MapWindow	MapSubwindows
UnmapWindow	UnmapSubwindows
ConfigureWindow	CirculateWindow
ChangeProperty	DeleteProperty
SendEvent	CreatePixmap
FreePixmap	CreateGC
ChangeGC	CopyGC
SetDashes	SetClipRectangles
FreeGC	ClearToBackground
PolyPoint	PolyLine
PolySegment	PolyRectangle
PolyArc	FillPolygon
PolyFillRectangle	PolyFillArc
PutImage	PolyText
ImageText8	ImageText16
CreateColormap	FreeColormap
InstallColormap	UninstallColormap
AllocColor	AllocNamedColor
AllocColorCells	FreeColors
StoreColors	

TABLE 2: *REPLACEMENT REQUESTS*

The following routines are implemented simply by calling the PanoramiX replacement function, which in turn calls wrapped `ScreenPtr`, `GCFunc`, and `GCOP` operations:

- `CopyPlane`
- `CopyArea`

In some cases, intercepting a request with the PanoramiX version and calling `SaveProc` for each screen creates extra replies to the client, which is not acceptable. The following routines have additional modifications to handle this situation:

- `ProcAllocColor`
- `ProcAllocNamedColor`
- `ProcAllocColorCells`

Prior to iteratively calling `ProcAllocColor`, `ProcAllocNamedColor`, or `ProcAlloc-ColorCells`, the `noPanoramiXExtension` flag is set to `False` if the colormap ID is not the real client ID. These routines check the **noPanoramiXExtension** flag before sending a reply to the client. This ensures a reply occurs only for the real client ID and not for fake PanoramiX client IDs.

WRAPPED FUNCTIONS

When the extension uses a GC to determine, for instance, the pixmap to use as part of a `CopyPlane` operation, that pixmap was created from within the X server itself, not from a client protocol request. The creation and modification of the GC must include iterations for each screen, so the resource routines can find it later. This involves wrapping the GCOps, GCFuncs, and `ScreenPtr` operations.

The following functions, defined in *xc/programs/Xserver/dix/dispatch.c*, wrap the GCOps operation so that it executes once for each physical screen:

- `CopyArea`
- `CopyPlane`
- `PolyPoint`
- `PolyLines`
- `PolySegment`
- `PolyRectangle`
- `PolyArc`
- `FillPolygon`
- `PolyFillRect`
- `PolyFillArc`
- `PolyText8`
- `PolyText16`

- `ImageText8`
- `ImageText16`

The following function wraps the `GCFuncs` operation:

- `ValidateGC`

And the following functions wrap the `ScreenPtr` operation:

- `CreateGC`
- `CreatePixmap`
- `UninstallColormap`
- `StoreColors`

These functions are very similar to their *mi-*, *cfb-*, or *ddx*-level equivalents, but they execute several times, each time substituting the appropriate resource IDs or pointers. Their implementation is to wrap the usual *ddx* function at GC creation or screen initialization, unwrap during execution so as to call the usual device-dependent function, and then rewrap at completion.

If there were a clean boundary between the device-independent and the device-dependent levels in the X server code, it is likely that these wrapped functions would not be needed. If the device-dependent level layer provided an interface for passing device information, then information to perform some operation could be set up in the device-independent layer. The PanoramiX Extension could then be implemented by merely enhancing that device-dependent layer to provide the requisite information *n* times. However, the reality is that the device-dependent layer frequently reaches back into the device-independent layer to derive pointers to needed information, or even to create structures, and in so doing needs to go through the iteration process itself.

These wrapped functions are exposed to a maintenance risk to a greater extent than the dispatch functions because their basic equivalents are less stable than the dispatch functions. Any changes made in the base functions must also be made in their wrapping functions.

REPLACEMENT FUNCTIONS

These functions are those that are not vectored by GC or `ScreenPtr`:

- `AllocColorCells`
- `ComputeFreezes`
- `FixUpEventFromWindow`
- `ProcessPointerEvent`
- `WriteEventsToClient`

The implementation of these functions consists of intervening into the base function with a test of `noPanoramiXExtension`. If PanoramiX is in use, flow transfers to an equivalent PanoramiX function and then returns.

Instead of defining new PanoramiX functions for the following resource routines, the routines have knowledge of the PanoramiX linked lists:

- `FreeResource`
- `FreeClientResources`
- `FreeResourceByType`
- `FreeClientNeverRetainResources`

As resources are freed, these routines are able to perform operations, such as marking an entry to free, on these linked lists.

EVENTS

Modifications were made so that a number of routines in */xc/programs/Xserver/dix/events.c* contain PanoramiX code changes.

`ComputeFreezes()`
> As part of processing pointer events, device events are delivered to clients that initiate grabs if an asynchronous pointer grab is in effect. Otherwise, `DeliverFocusEvent` is called to search for one or more clients interested in the event. This routine is modified to adjust the values passed to `XYToWindow` such that `xE->u.keyButtonPointer.rootX` and `xE->u.keyButtonPointer.rootX` represent the position of the event on the one large screen. The routine also forces window IDs to real client IDs for any events delivered to clients.

`FixUpEventFromWindow()`
> This routine was modified to use a window pointer derived from a real client window ID. This requires a search through the PanoramiX window linked list for the matching window ID.

`WarpPointer()`
> This routine was changed to determine the location of the cursor by calculating screen boundaries based on PanoramiX data width and height values. Using this known screen location, the destination `x` and `y` values are adjusted by the screen's `PanoramiXData` `x` and `y` information.

`ProcessPointerEvent()`
> This routine was modified to adjust the cursor's `x` and `y` values, which is done by first searching for the window ID in the PanoramiX window linked list. When a match is found, the corresponding `x`, `y` data is known, and an x and y offset is calculated. This offset is then used to produce the accurate `rootX` and `rootY` values for the event

`GrabPointer()`
> This routine modifies the `confinedTo` window value to a PanoramiX window ID if the `confinedTo` window value is not the `RootWindow`. If a match is found, for each screen the routine searches for the location of the confined window's top-left

corner. Based on the window's coordinates, the routine chooses the window that is actually seen. If the window is not realized or if the region is not empty, the routine passes this window to activate a grab.

`QueryPointer()`

This routine was modified to reply with `winX`, `winY`, `rootX`, and `rootY` values that are adjusted by PanoramiX data information based on the screen the pointer resides in.

`CheckDeviceGrabs()`

This routine was changed to modify the pointer event. It is necessary to search the PanoramiX window linked list for a matching window ID and then iterate through each screen calling `CheckPassiveGrabsOnWindow` with the appropriate PanoramiX window ID.

`SetInputFocus()`

This routine gets called by `ProcSetInputFocus`. Since `stuff->focus` can contain only client-known IDs, this would always cause the input focus to be constrained to `screen0`. This routine was modified to get the physical screen number for the cursor. The routine passes the corresponding PanoramiX window ID, rather than the client window ID to the `SetInputFocus` routine.

`GetInputFocus()`

Similar to `SetInputFocus`, this routine determines the appropriate PanoramiX window ID based on the physical screen number of the cursor.

`WriteEventsToClient()`

`WriteEventsToClient` checks the type of event being sent to the client and either forces the event to use a real client ID and send the event or skips a fake ID and returns.

The following events loop for each physical screen and force the window ID to a real window ID, so that they never send a PanoramiX fake ID to a client:

- `ButtonPress`
- `ButtonRelease`
- `MotionNotify`
- `KeyPress`
- `EnterNotify`
- `LeaveNotify`
- `Expose`

The events in Table 3 contain one or more window IDs described by variables like `parent`, `window`, `sibling`, `aboveSibling`, and `drawable`.

FocusOut	FocusIn
VisibilityNotify	GraphicsExpose
CreateNotify	ColormapNotify
MapNotify	DestroyNotify
GravityNotify	MapRequest
ConfigureNotify	ConfigureRequest
ResizeRequest	CirculateNotify
CirculateRequest	ReparentNotify
PropertyNotify	ClientMessage

TABLE 3: *EVENTS THAT CONTAIN WINDOW IDs*

When one of these events are encountered, the routine skips fake IDs and `WriteEvent-sToClient` returns to the calling routine.

RESOURCES

Currently, PanoramiX linked lists are cleaned up in `CloseDownClient` and in `NextAvailableClient`, which is where `FreeClientResources` is called. This seemed like the best time to make sure there are no stray PanoramiX entries. If PanoramiX linked list entries aren't removed, it is possible to get duplicate IDs in a list. The entries are marked when resources are freed, but PanoramiX ID entries are not actually freed until all of the resources for a given client have been freed.

The actual code changes appear as follows:

```
#ifdef PANORAMIX
    PanoramiXGC *pPanoramiXGC;
    PanoramiXGC *pPanoramiXGCback = NULL;
    PanoramiXWindow  *pPanoramiXWin;
    PanoramiXWindow  *pPanoramiXWinback = NULL;
    PanoramiXCmap *pPanoramiXCmap;
    PanoramiXCmap *pPanoramiXCmapback = NULL;
    PanoramiXPmap *pPanoramiXPmap;
    PanoramiXPmap *pPanoramiXPmapback = NULL;
#endif
    FreeClientResources(client);

#ifdef PANORAMIX
    PanoramiX_FREE(client);
#endif
```

When `FreeClientResources`, defined in */xc/programs/Xserver/dix/resource.c*, is called, all resources associated with the client are freed.

FONTS

The `doPolyText` routine in */xc/programs/Xserver/dix/dixfonts.c* was modified to check the `noPanoramiXExtension` flag to control when errors are sent to the client. If a check is not added to this routine, extra error replies based on non-client resource IDs would be written to the client. The client would not recognize these IDs because they are created by the extension. The flag is set to `True` in the `PanoramiXPolyText` function if the window is not the real ID requested by the client.

SERVER EXTENSIONS

Extensions that manipulate window and screen pointers based on client window IDs need to know about PanoramiX data structures. These extensions must be modified to perform graphics operations in an interative fashion to support PanoramiX.

SHAPE

The current implementation works with a modified version of the Shape Extension. The `ConfineToShape()` routine in *cursor.h* was changed to give it exposure outside of the device-independent layer. In addition, the following routines were intercepted at `ProcShapeDispatch()` in *shape.c*:

- `ProcShapeRectangles`
- `ProcShapeMask`
- `ProcShapeCombine`
- `ProcShapeOffset`

DPS EXTENSION

Displaying a PostScript file on an X server running with the PanoramiX extension currently does not work properly. Modifications to the DPS Extension will be necessary and might be difficult to integrate into the current code base.

CONCLUSIONS

Digital has successfully implemented the PanoramiX Extension for the X11 Release 6 X server to support a multi-headed single root window. This implementation has been accomplished at the device-independence level, which has the advantage that no low-level graphics code changes are required, which means less maintenance of the extension.

The current implementation is a very simple approach and as such has very few places for introducing drawing errors. Some of the limitations are that X server extensions require modifications to work with the PanoramiX extension. Another issue is that the extension does not support a query to get the dimensions of the logical screen; this capability is planned for a future release.

Another problem area is performance. Drawing duplicate windows and pixmaps for each screen can be expensive and is expected to slow performance and consume more memory. As the number of heads on a workstation increases, the performance is likely to deteriorate, and memory consumption will increase. These issues will be addressed in a future release. Some ideas for the future include using a single window or pixmap for each screen, instead of creating duplicate windows and pixmaps.

ACKNOWLEDGMENTS

Don Haney, an employee of Digital Equipment Corporation, provided the original design and initial implementation. I am very thankful that he left this project to me and forever grateful for his wisdom and guidance. Thanks to Rob Lembree and Will Walker for suggesting I write this paper. Special thanks to Irene McCartney, Rob Lembree, and Will Walker who took the time to read this paper and suggest changes to earlier versions.

REFERENCES

[Jones94] Jones, Peter C. "Xvan: A True Multiple Screen X Server, An Implementation Overview." THE X RESOURCE 9 (1994).

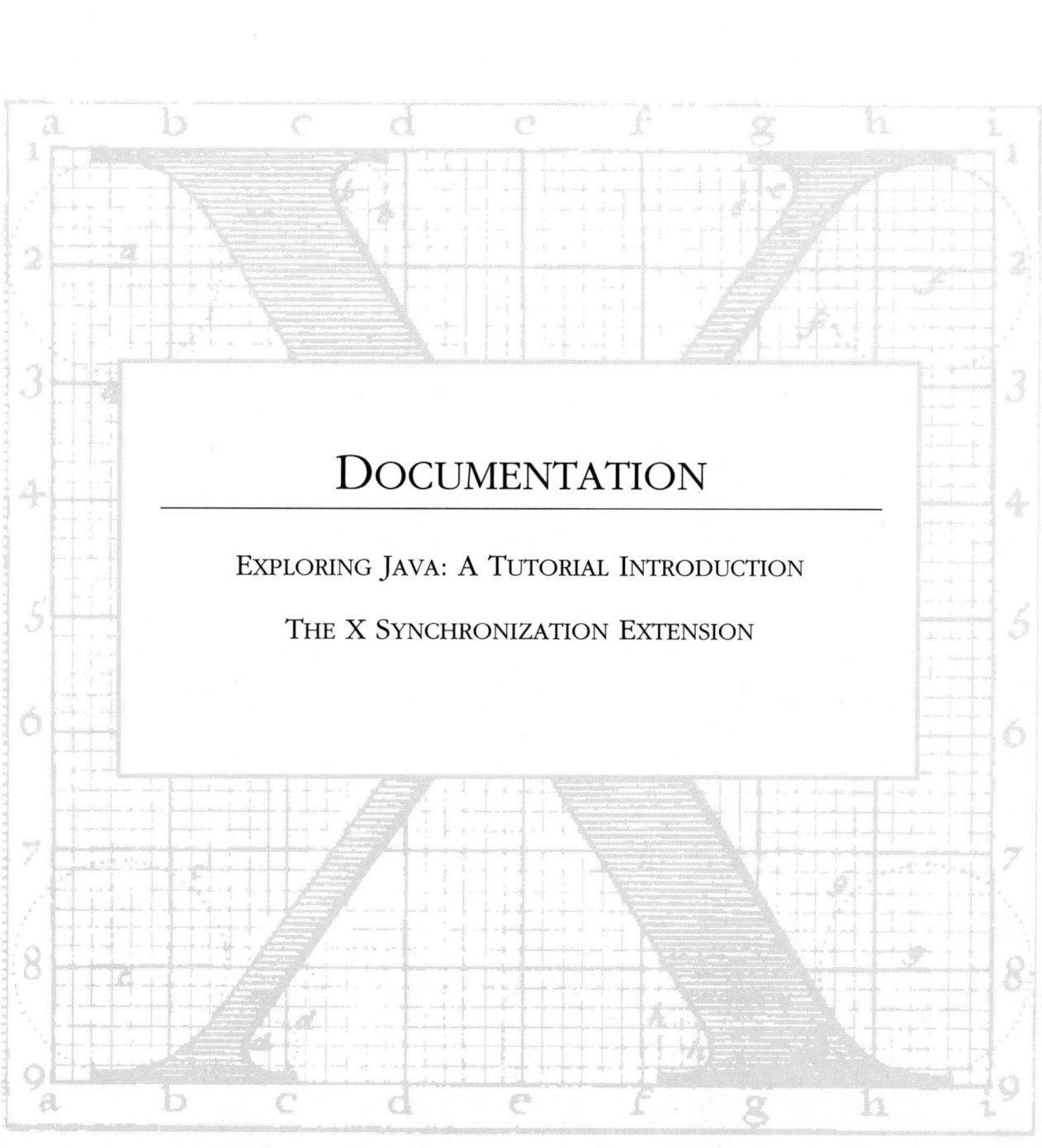

DOCUMENTATION

EXPLORING JAVA: A TUTORIAL INTRODUCTION

THE X SYNCHRONIZATION EXTENSION

Exploring Java

A Tutorial Introduction

Pat Niemeyer

Introducing Java

The Java programming language, developed at Sun Microsystems, is a truly machine-independent programming language. Java applications, including Web applications known as *applets*, are safe enough to traverse networks and powerful enough to replace native executable code. Tools powered by Java have the potential to change the Net from a patchwork of information "islands" into a unified, distributed computing environment with an evolving library of tools and resources. Java has captured the imagination of many people and is one of the most eagerly anticipated "standards" that the Net community has seen. It has the potential to change the way a lot of people think about software.

Java began life in 1992 as a language called Oak, developed by Sun for "information appliances" such as personal digital assistants (PDAs), cellular phones, and "set top" interactive television boxes. It was small, robust, architecture-independent, and object oriented. As it happens, these are also the requirements for a universal, network-savvy programming language, and that is what Java has become.

Java derives much of its form and philosophy from C and C++; if you are familiar with those languages, you'll feel right at home. Java is a compiled language. However, whereas C and C++ code is compiled directly to native machine code, Java is compiled to instructions for a virtual machine. Compiled Java "byte code" is an architecture-independent, binary format that executes on any platform that implements the Java run-time system. It is this intermediate layer—the virtual machine—that makes Java portable and safe. Java byte-code is interpreted, but it has been designed so that it can be compiled to native machine code "on the fly." This means that Java code can be almost as fast as native code, while maintaining important safety features.

---

*Pat Niemeyer (**pat@pat.net**) is a full-time member of Europa Design Group, LLC, where he consults on projects involving distributed applications, object oriented design, and language development. The following tutorial is an excerpt from the forthcoming book, **Exploring Java**, by Pat Niemeyer and Josh Peck, from O'Reilly & Associates.*

Three features are essential to support a universal language today: portability, speed, and security. You will no doubt hear a tremendous amount about the fact that Java is a "safe" language. What do we mean by safe? Safe from whom? Well, safe from others, of course, but just as importantly, safe from ourselves, as well as from sloppy software vendors and the contractor down the hall.

First, Java is a strongly typed language. The Java compiler does as much type checking and usage analysis as possible at compile time, allowing many flaws to be caught early in the design cycle. Java is fully run-time typed as well, allowing safe incremental development and late binding with code that your compiler has never seen.

Next, the Java language itself has a few well-chosen concessions and simplifications that make the virtual environment more powerful and, as we shall see, verifiable. The most obvious differences between Java and C and C++ are the addition of garbage collection and true arrays, and the absence of ad-hoc pointers. These changes remove many problems with safety, portability, and optimization. Garbage collection alone should save a generation of programmers from a large source of programmer error: explicit memory management. Arrays in Java are true "first-class" objects, eliminating situations that call for pointer arithmetic and the juggling of memory. Pointers in Java are replaced by `refer-ences`, which are strongly typed "handles" for objects. All objects in Java, with the exception of simple numeric types, are accessed through references.

Java is quite parsimonious in its features. Some features that have been troublesome in other languages have been replaced in Java. For example, Java supports only single class inheritance but allows multiple inheritance of interfaces. Interfaces, like abstract classes, specify the behavior of a class without forcing an implementation. This mechanism is borrowed from Objective C. Like a class, an `interface` in Java can serve as a type. As a result, it is possible to write methods that can accept any object that implements a particular behavior and avoid coupling code to a particular part of the inheritance hierarchy.

Java's roots are in networked devices and embedded systems. For these applications, it is important to have robust and proactive error management. Java has an exception mechanism somewhat like that being considered for C++. Methods in Java are required to declare the exceptions that they can signal or, alternatively, catch and deal with the errors themselves. Thus, the Java programmer knows precisely what exceptional conditions he or she must deal with and has help from the compiler in writing correct software that does not leave them unhandled.

It is one thing to create a language that prevents you from shooting yourself in the foot, but it is quite another to create one that prevents others from shooting you in the foot. Before execution, Java byte-code is passed through a "verifier" that attempts to make guarantees about how the code will behave. Verified code cannot forge pointers or violate access permissions on objects. It cannot perform illegal casts or use objects in ways other than the ways they are intended to be used. It cannot even generate certain types of internal errors such as overflowing the operand stack. These claims are what makes it possible to dynamically download code from an untrusted source over the Net and let it run alongside your confidential information.

Applications today require a high degree of parallelism, but it is not enough just to add concurrency to a language. Managing the synchronization of threads can be tricky and providing for robust error handling is difficult without explicit language support. Java is multithreaded, with language-level support for synchronization based on the "monitor and condition" model. Java uses a keyword, `synchronized`, to lock a class for safe, exclusive access among specified methods.

The concept of universal executable content is very exciting; it is more than just a new way of writing applications. Java should make possible a variety of new applications that were not feasible before, including new models of software distribution and interoperability. For example, Sun's HotJava Web browser, which is written entirely in Java, is dynamically extensible through *content handlers* and *protocol handlers*. Suppose that I create a new image format. I can also create a content handler in Java that understands this new format and place it on my Web server along with my images. The first time someone points his or her Java-savvy browser at my site, the browser will realize that it does not understand the new format and will ask the server if a content handler exists for it. Since there is a content handler, the browser seamlessly upgrades itself to handle the new format.

As of this writing, a beta version of Java called the Java Developers Kit (JDK) is available for the following platforms:

- Sparc Solaris (2.3 or higher)
- Windows NT
- Windows 95

If you want to try out the examples in this tutorial and write your own applets, you'll need to get the latest release from *http://java.sun.com*. Netscape Navigator 2.0, which is also available as a beta release, supports Java applets, so you can use it to view Java in action. For more information about this release of Netscape, see *http://home.netscape.com*.

This tutorial is designed to provide a crash course on some of the basic features of Java. The examples and discussion that follow do not cover all of the functionality of Java. Instead, they provide a taste of the tools and techniques used to write Java applets. If this article whets your appetite for more information, you'll need to consult the various online resources. You may also want to subscribe to the *comp.lang.java* newsgroup to keep up with current developments.

HELLO WEB!

In the tradition of all good introductory programming texts, we begin with Java's equivalent of the archetypal "Hello World" application. In the spirit of our new world, we'll call it "Hello Web!".

We'll take three passes at this example, adding features and introducing new concepts along the way. First, let's get our minimalist version running:

```
public class HelloWeb extends java.applet.Applet {

        public void paint( java.awt.Graphics gc ) {
                gc.drawString("Hello Web!", 125, 95 );
        }

}
```

Place the text of this example in a file called *HelloWeb.java*. Now compile this source:

```
% javac HelloWeb.java
```

This produces the Java byte-code binary class file *HelloWeb.class*.

Now we need an HTML document that contains the appropriate `applet` tag to display our example. Place the following text in a file called *HelloWeb.html* in the same directory as the binary class file:

```
<html>
<head>
        <title>Example</title>
</head>
<body>
        <applet code=HelloWeb width=300 height=200></applet>
</body>
</html>
```

Finally, we can point our Java-enabled Web browser at this document with a URL such as:

```
http://yourServer/wherever/HelloWeb.html
```

or

```
file:/wherever/HelloWeb.html
```

Now you should see the proclamation shown in Figure 1.

Congratulations, you have written your first applet! Take a moment to bask in the glow of your monitor.

HelloWeb may be a small program, but actually quite a bit is going on behind the scenes. Those five lines represent just the tip of an iceberg. What lies under the surface are layers of functionality provided by the Java language and its foundation class libraries. In this tutorial, I will cover a lot of ground quickly in an effort to show you the "big picture." I will try to offer enough detail for a complete understanding of what is happening in each example but avoid exhaustive explanations. This holds for both elements of the Java language and the object oriented concepts that apply to them.

CLASSES

The previous example defines a *class* named `HelloWeb`. Classes are the fundamental building blocks of most object oriented languages. They are containers that hold variables and methods (functions) pertaining to a logical component of an application. Such a

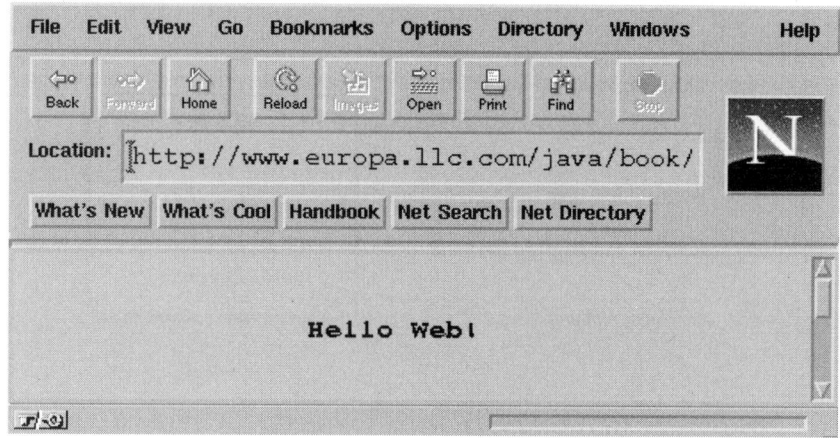

FIGURE 1: *HELLO WEB! APPLET*

component might be something concrete, such as a button on a screen or the information in a spreadsheet, or it could be something more abstract, such as a sorting algorithm or possibly the sense of ennui in your MUD character. In each case, the class contains variables that hold the state (data) of the component and methods that implement its behavior. A hypothetical spreadsheet class might, for example, have variables that represent the value of its individual cells and methods that perform operations on those cells, such as "clear a row" or "compute values."

Our `HelloWeb` class is the container for our Java application. It holds two general types of variables and methods; those that we need for our specific applications' tasks and some special "predesignated" ones that we provide in order to interact with the outside world. The Java run-time environment and a Java-enabled Web browser periodically call methods in `HelloWeb` to pass us information and prod us to perform actions, as depicted in Figure 2. Our simple `HelloWeb` class defines a single method called `paint()`. The `paint()` method is called by Java when it is time for our application to draw itself on the screen.

You will see that the `HelloWeb` class derives some of its structure from another class called `Applet`. This is why we refer to `HelloWeb` as an "applet."

CLASS INSTANCES AND OBJECTS

Classes contain methods and variables that represent particular things. Many individual run-time representations (working copies) of a given class can be in existence while an application is active. These individual incarnations are called *instances* of the class. Two instances of a given class may contain different states (data) but always have the same methods. As an example, consider a `Button` class. There is only one `Button` class, but many actual working instances of "buttons" can be in an application. Furthermore, two `Button` instances might contain different data, perhaps giving each a different appear-

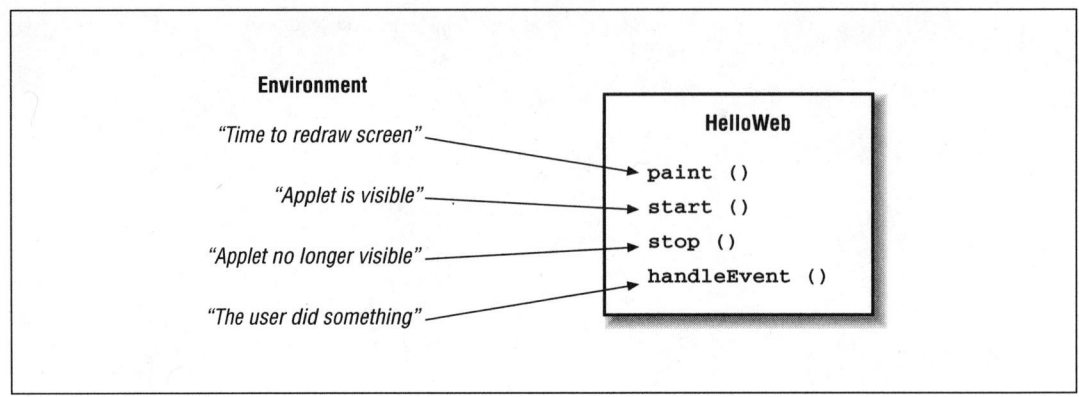

FIGURE 2: *METHOD INVOCATION IN THE JAVA ENVIRONMENT*

ance or specifying a different message for each to send when it is pressed. In this sense, a class can be considered a "mold" for making the objects that it represents; something like a cookie cutter stamping out working instances of itself in the memory of the computer.

The term *object* is very general and in some other contexts is used almost interchangeably with class. Objects are the abstract entities that all object oriented languages refer to in one form or another. I will use object as a generic term for an instance of a class. I might, therefore, refer to an instance of the `Button` class as a `Button`, a `Button` object, or, indiscriminately, as an object.

A Java-enabled Web browser creates an instance of our `HelloWeb` class when our applet is first used. If we had included the `HelloWeb applet` tag in our HTML document twice (causing it to appear twice on the screen), the browser would have created and managed two separate `HelloWeb` objects (two separate instances of the `HelloWeb` class).

VARIABLES

Classes can contain variables of various types. In Java, every class defines a new type. A variable can be declared to be of this type and can then "hold" instances of that class. A variable could, for example, be of type `Button` and hold an instance of the `Button` class, or of type `SpreadSheetCell` and hold a `SpreadSheetCell` object, just as it could be one of any of the more familiar types such as `integer` or `float`. In this way, by having variables containing complex objects, a class may use other classes as tools within itself. Using classes in this way is called *composition*. Our examples in this tutorial are somewhat unrealistic in that we are building only a single class of our own. However, we will be using many classes as tools within our applet.

You have seen only one variable used so far in our simple `HelloWeb` example. It is found in the declaration of our lonely `paint()` method:

```
public void paint( java.awt.Graphics gc ) {
```

Just like functions in C (and many other languages), a method in Java declares a list of variables that are to hold its arguments, and it specifies the types of those arguments. Our `paint()` method takes one argument named (somewhat tersely) `gc`, which is of type `Graphics` class. When the `paint()` method is invoked, a `Graphics` object is assigned to `gc`, which we use in the body of the method. More about `paint()` and the `Graphics` class in a moment.

A WORD ABOUT VARIABLES

I have loosely referred to variables as "holding" objects. In reality, variables that have complex types (class types) don't so much "contain" objects as "point" to them. Class type variables are references to objects. A reference is a pointer to or another name for an object.

This means that the declaration of a variable does not imply that any storage is necessarily allocated for that variable or that an instance of its type even exists anywhere. When a class type variable is first declared, it has the value **NULL**, meaning "no value." Before it can be used, it must be assigned to an actual instance of an appropriate class. It then becomes a reference to (another name for) that object.

This begs the question of where we get an instance of a class to assign to a variable in the first place. The answer, as we will see later, is through the use of the **new** operator. In our first two passes at this example, we are dealing only with objects that are handed to us "prefabricated" from somewhere outside of our class. Later, we will examine object creation.

INHERITANCE

Java classes are arranged in a parent-child hierarchy, in which the parent and child are known as the superclass and subclass, respectively. In Java, every class has exactly one superclass (a single parent) but possibly many subclasses.

The declaration of our class in the previous example uses the keyword **extends** to specify that `HelloWeb` is a subclass of the `Applet` class.

```
public class HelloWeb extends java.applet.Applet {
```

A subclass may be allowed to inherit some or all of the variables and methods of its superclass. Through *inheritance*, the subclass can use those members as if it had declared them itself. A subclass can add variables and methods of its own, and it can also override the meaning of inherited variables and methods. When we use a subclass, overridden variables and methods are completely hidden (replaced) by the subclass' own version of them. In this way, inheritance provides a powerful mechanism whereby a subclass may build upon its superclass and "refine" or "extend" it.

The hypothetical spreadsheet class might be subclassed to produce a new scientific spreadsheet class, with extra mathematical functions and special built-in constants. In this case, the source code for the scientific spreadsheet might declare methods for the added mathematical functions and variables for the special constants, but the new class automatically has all of the variables and methods that constitute the normal functionality of a spreadsheet; they are inherited from the parent spreadsheet class. This means that the scientific spreadsheet maintains its identity as a spreadsheet, and we can continue to use it anywhere that we could use the basic spreadsheet.

Our `HelloWeb` class is a subclass of the `Applet` class and inherits many variables and methods that we do not see explicitly declared in our source code. These members function in exactly the same way as the ones that we add or override.

APPLET

The `Applet` class is the framework for building applets. It contains methods that provide the basic functionality for a Java application that can be displayed and controlled by a Java-enabled Web browser or other Java-enabled software. Methods of the `Applet` class are overridden by subclasses to implement the behavior of a particular applet. This may sound restrictive, as if we are limited to some predefined set of routines, but this is not the case at all. Keep in mind that the methods we are talking about are mainly means of getting information from the outside world. A realistic application might involve hundreds or even thousands of classes, with legions of methods and variables and multiple threads of execution. The vast majority of these are related to the particulars of our job. The inherited methods of the `Applet` class and of other special components simply serve as a framework on which we can "hang" code to handle certain types of events and perform special tasks.

The `paint()` method is an important method of the `Applet` class that we override to implement the way in which our particular applet displays itself on the screen. The other inherited members of `Applet` that we do not override provide basic functionality and reasonable defaults for this (trivial) example. As `HelloWeb` grows we will delve deeper into the inherited members and override additional methods. They will allow us to get information from the user and give us more control over what our applet does. We will also be adding some arbitrary, application-specific methods and variables for the needs of `HelloWeb`.

RELATIONSHIPS AND "FINGER POINTING"

We can correctly refer to `HelloWeb` as an `Applet` because subclassing can be thought of as creating an "is-a" relationship, in which the subclass is a kind of its superclass. `HelloWeb` is therefore a kind of `Applet`. When we refer to a kind of object, we mean any instance of that object's class and any of its subclasses. Later, we will look more closely at the Java class hierarchy and see that `Applet` is itself a subclass of the `Panel` class, which is further derived from a class called `Container`, and so on, as shown in Figure 3.

In this sense, an `Applet` is a kind of `Panel`, which is, itself, a kind of `Container` and each of these can ultimately be considered to be a kind of `Component`. We will see later that it is from these classes that `Applet` inherits its basic graphical user interface functionality and the ability to have other graphical components embedded within it.

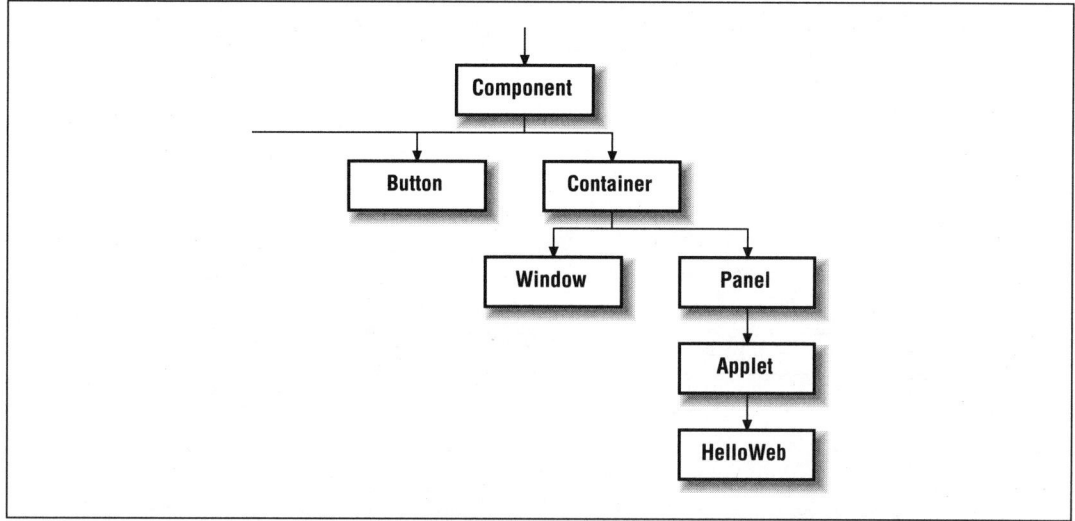

FIGURE 3: *PART OF THE JAVA CLASS HIERARCHY*

The direction of the arrows in Figure 3 is really a matter of semantics. We are emphasizing subclassing; however, you will often see arrows pointing in the opposite direction (up toward the superclass), in which case they are following the flow of the is-a relationship. Arrows are just arrows.

PACKAGES

In our example, the `Applet` class is referenced by its fully qualified name `java.applet.Applet`.

```
public class HelloWeb extends java.applet.Applet {
```

The prefix on the class name identifies it as belonging to the `java.applet` *package*. Packages provide a means of organizing Java classes. A package is a group of Java classes that are related by purpose or by application. Classes in the same package can have special access privileges with respect to one another and may be designed to work together. Package names are hierarchical and are intended to be used somewhat like Internet domain and host names, to distinguish groups of classes by organization and application. Classes can be dynamically loaded over networks from arbitrary locations; within this context packages provide a crude namespace of Java classes.[†]

---

† There are many efforts underway to find general solutions to the problem of locating resources in a globally distributed computing environment. The Universal Resource Identifier Working Group of the IETF has proposed "Universal Resource Names." A URN would be a more abstract and persistent identifier that would be resolved to a URL through the use of a name service. One can imagine a day when a global namespace of trillions of persistent objects will exist, forming the infrastructure for all of our computing resources. Java provides an important evolutionary step in this direction.

`java.applet` identifies a particular package which contains classes related to applets. `java.applet.Applet` identifies a specific class, the `Applet` class, within that package. The `java.` hierarchy is special. Any package that begins with `java.` is part of the core Java API and is available on any platform that supports Java. Figure 4 illustrates the core Java packages, showing a representative class or two from each package.

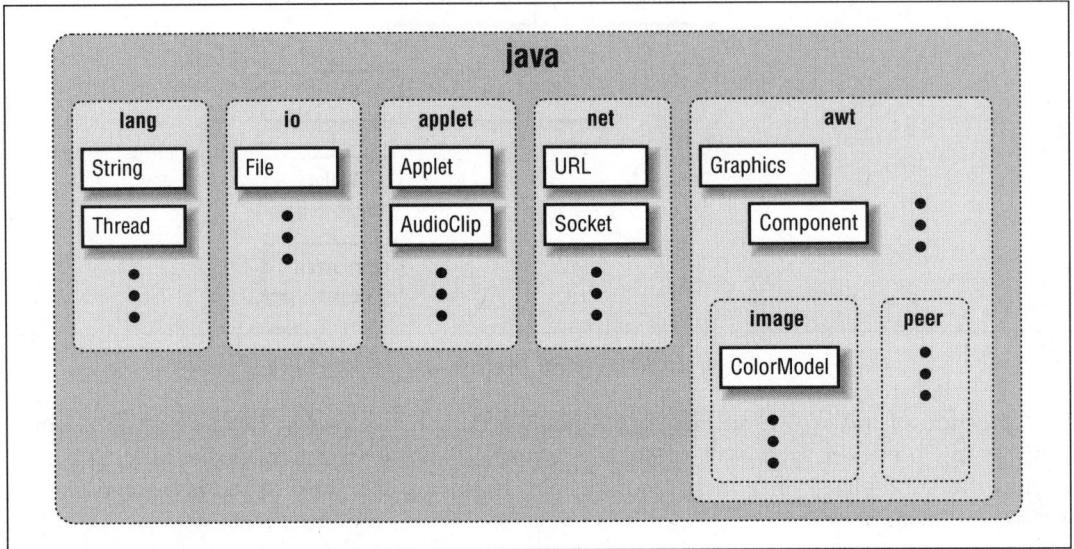

FIGURE 4: *THE CORE JAVA PACKAGES*

Some notable core packages include: `java.lang`, which contains fundamental classes needed by the Java language itself; `java.awt`, which contains classes of the Java Abstract Windowing Toolkit; and `java.net`, which contains the networking classes.

A few classes contain methods that are not written in Java but instead are part of the native Java implementation on a particular platform. Approximately 22 such classes are in the `java.` package hierarchy; these are the only classes that ever have to be ported to a new platform. They form the basis for all interaction with the operating system. All other classes are built on or around these and are completely platform independent.

THE PAINT( ) METHOD

The source for our `HelloWeb` class defines just one method, `paint()`, which overrides the `paint()` method from the Applet class.

```
public void paint( java.awt.Graphics gc ) {
        gc.drawString("Hello Web!", 125, 95 );
}
```

The `paint()` method is called by Java when it is time for our applet to draw itself on the screen. It takes a single argument, a `Graphics` object, and returns no type of value (void) to its caller.

The `Graphics` object (an instance of the `Graphics` class) represents a particular graphical drawing area and is also called a "graphics context." It contains methods that the applet can use to draw in this area and variables that represent characteristics such as clipping or drawing modes. The particular `Graphics` object that we are passed in the `paint()` method corresponds to our applet's area of the screen.

The `Graphics` class provides methods for rendering primitive shapes, images, and text. In `HelloWeb`, we invoke the `drawString()` method of our `Graphics` object to scrawl our message at the specified coordinates.

ACCESSING METHODS AND VARIABLES

As in C++, methods and variables of an object are accessed in a hierarchical way by appending their names with "`.`" (dots) to the objects that hold them. We invoked the `drawString()` method of the `Graphics` object, referenced by our `gc` variable, in this way:

```
gc.drawString( arguments ... );
```

Modifiers are keywords placed before classes, variables, and methods to alter their accessibility, behavior, or semantics. `paint()` is declared as `public`, which means that the method can be invoked (called) by methods in classes other than `HelloWeb`. In this case, it is the Java windowing environment that is calling our `paint()` method. A method or variable declared as `private` is inaccessible from outside of its class.

HELLOWEB! II: THE SEQUEL

Let's make our applet a little more interactive, shall we? The following improvement, `HelloWeb2`, allows us to drag the message around with the mouse. `HelloWeb2` is also customizable. It takes the text of its message from a parameter of the `applet` tag in the HTML document.

`HelloWeb2` is a new applet—another subclass of the `Applet` class. In that sense, it is a sibling of `HelloWeb`. Having just seen inheritance at work, you might wonder why we aren't creating a subclass of `HelloWeb` and exploiting inheritance to build upon our previous example and extend its functionality. Well, in this case, that would not necessarily be an advantage, and for clarity we simply start over.[†] Here is `HelloWeb2`:

---

† You are left to consider whether such a subclassing arrangement would even make sense. Should HelloWeb2 really be a "kind-of" HelloWeb? Are we looking for refinement or just code re-use?

```
import java.applet.Applet;
import java.awt.*;

public class HelloWeb2 extends Applet {
        int messageX = 125, messageY = 95;
        String theMessage;

        public void init() {
                theMessage = getParameter("message");
        }

        public void paint( Graphics gc ) {
                gc.drawString( theMessage, messageX, messageY );
        }

        public boolean mouseDrag(Event evt, int x, int y ) {
                messageX = x;
                messageY = y;
                repaint();
                return true;
        }
}
```

Place the text of this example in a file called *HelloWeb2.java,* and compile it as before. You should get a new class file *HelloWeb2.class* as a result. We also need to create a new `applet` tag for `HelloWeb2`. You can either create another HTML document (copy *HelloWeb.html* and modify it) or simply add a second `applet` tag to the existing *HelloWeb.html* file. The `applet` tag for `HelloWeb2` has to use a parameter; it should look something like:

```
<applet code=HelloWeb2 width=300 height=200>
<param name="message" value="Hello Web!" >
</applet>
```

Feel free to substitute your own salacious comment for the value of message.

Run this applet in your Java-enabled Web browser, and enjoy many hours of fun, dragging the text around with your mouse.

IMPORT

So, what have we added? First you may notice that a couple of lines are now hovering above our class:

```
import java.applet.Applet;
import java.awt.*;

public class HelloWeb2 extends Applet {
    ...
```

The `import` statement lists external classes that we want to use in this file (or compilation unit to be politically correct) and tells the compiler where to look for them. In our first `HelloWeb` example, we designated the `Applet` class as the superclass of `HelloWeb`. Since `Applet` was not defined by us, the compiler had to look elsewhere for it. In that case, we referred to `Applet` by its fully qualified name, `java.applet.Applet`, which told the compiler that `Applet` belongs to the `java.applet` package so it knew where to find it.

The `import` statement is simply a convenience. By importing `java.applet.Applet` in this example, we tell the compiler up front that we are using this class and, thereafter in this file, we can simply refer to it as `Applet`. The second `import` statement makes use of the wildcard ".*" to tell the compiler to import all of the classes in the `java.awt` package. But don't worry, the compiled code does not contain any excess baggage. Java doesn't do things like that. In fact, compiled Java classes don't "contain" other classes at all. They simply note their relationships. Our example only uses the `java.awt.Graphics` class. However, we are anticipating using several more classes from this package in the next examples.

The `import` statement may seem a bit like the C or C++ preprocessor `#include` statement, which is primarily used to inject header files into programs at the appropriate places. This is not true. There are no header files in Java. Unlike compiled C or C++ libraries, Java binary class files contain all of the necessary type information about the classes, methods, and variables that they contain, obviating the need for prototyping.

INSTANCE VARIABLES

We have added some variables to our example:

```
public class HelloWeb2 extends Applet {
    int messageX = 125, messageY = 95;
    String theMessage;

    ...
```

`messageX` and `messageY` are integers that hold the current coordinates of our movable message. They are initialized to default values, which should place a message of our length somewhere near the center of the applet. Java integers are always 32-bit signed numbers. You needn't fret about what architecture your code is running on; numeric types in Java are precisely defined.

The variable `theMessage` is of type `String` and can "hold" instances of the `String` class. Unless otherwise initialized, instance variables are set to a default value of 0 (zero) or `NULL`. Numeric types are set to zero; class type variables always have their values set to

NULL, which means "no value." Attempting to use an object with a NULL value results in a run-time error.

You should note that these three variables are declared inside the braces of the class definition but not inside any particular method in that class. These variables are called *instance variables* because they belong to the entire class and copies of them appear in each separate instance of the class. Instance variables are always visible (usable) in any of the methods inside their classes. Depending on their modifiers, they may also be accessible from outside of the class.

Methods

We have made some changes to our previously stodgy paint() method. All of the arguments in the call to Graphics.drawString() are now variables.

Two new methods have appeared in our class. Like paint(), these are methods of the base Applet class that we are overriding to add our own functionality. init() is an important method of the Applet class. It is called once, when our applet is created, to give us an opportunity to do any work that is needed to "set up shop". init() is a good place to allocate resources and perform other activities that need happen only once in the lifetime of the Applet.

An important concept that we will come to a bit later is that of the *constructor*. Constructors are special methods of a class that serve to help "set up" and initialize an instance of a class when it is first created. The init() method of the Applet class serves a very similar purpose; however, it is different. Constructors are a feature of the Java language. All classes, including Applet, have constructors. init(), however, is just a method of the Applet class like any other. It is an application-level phenomenon. A Java-enabled Web browser calls init() when it prepares to place the Applet on a page. If we were running an applet outside of the context of a Web browser, we would be creating an instance of an Applet and calling its init() method.

Our overridden init() method does just one thing; it sets the text of the theMessage instance variable:

```
public void init() {
        theMessage = getParameter("message");
}
```

When an applet is instantiated, the parameters given in the applet tag of the HTML document are stored in a table and made available to us through the getParameter() method. Given the name of a parameter, it returns the value as a String object. If the name is not found, it returns a NULL value.

So what, you may ask, is the type of the argument to the getParameter() method? It, too, is a String. With a little magic from the Java compiler, quoted strings in the source code are turned into String objects. A bit of funny business is going on here, but it is simply for convenience.

`getParameter()` is a public method that we inherited from the `Applet` class. We could use it from any of our methods. Note that the `getParameter()` method is invoked directly by name; no object name is prepended to it with a dot. If a method exists in our class (or is inherited from a superclass), we can call it directly by name. In addition, we can use a special read-only variable, called `this`, to explicitly refer to "our" object. A method can use `this` to refer to the instance of the object that holds it. The following two statements are therefore equivalent:

```
theMessage = getParameter("message");
```

or

```
theMessage = this.getParameter("message");
```

We'll always use the shorter form. We will need the `this` variable later when we have to pass a reference to "our" object to a method in another class. We often do this so that methods in another class can give us a call back at some future time or watch our public variables.

EVENTS

The last bit of the HelloWeb2 example is the method we have added to get information from the mouse. Each time the user performs an action, such as hitting a key on the keyboard, moving the mouse, or perhaps banging his or her head against a touch-sensitive screen, Java generates an *event*. An event represents an action that has occurred; it contains information about the action, such as its time and location. Events can usually be associated with a particular graphical user interface component of an application. A keystroke, for instance, might correspond to a character being typed into a text entry field. Pressing a mouse button might cause a graphical button on the screen to activate. Even just moving the mouse within a certain area of the screen might be intended to trigger effects such as highlighting or changing to a special mouse cursor.

Every area of "real-estate" on the screen belongs to some GUI component, which may be designed to respond to different types of events within its boundaries. Components are graphical entities, which are managed by a Java object. In each case, Java determines to which component the action belongs and delivers the event to the appropriate object. Information about an event is wrapped up in an instance of the `java.awt.Event` class and delivered by invoking a method in the receiving object. The `Event` object is passed as an argument to that method.

In this example, our `Applet` serves as the single component to which events are delivered. The `mouseDrag()` method is one of a suite of routines that we can override to handle specific types of events when they are delivered to us:

```
public boolean mouseDrag(Event evt, int x, int y ) {
        messageX = x;
        messageY = y;
        repaint();
        return true;
}
```

As the mouse is dragged, Java calls the `mouseDrag()` method repeatedly to update us on its position. Each invocation of `mouseDrag()` corresponds to a discrete position of the mouse.

The first argument to `mouseDrag()` is the `Event` object that contains information about this event. We assign the `Event` to the `evt` variable. It contains, among other things, data specifying the type of event (mouse movement), the component in which it happened (our applet), and the x,y coordinates of the event (the current mouse position). The last two arguments to `mouseDrag()` are integers which, redundantly, contain the x,y coordinates of the mouse position.

This may seem a bit confusing. If the `Event` object has all of the information, why do we have a specific method for this type of event, and why are we passed the x,y coordinates in separate variables? The answer is that `mouseDrag()` is a programming convenience. A lower level method looks at the `Event` first and, based on its type, dispatches it to one of several more specific methods. In this case, we do not have to bother with the `Event` argument to `mouseDrag()`, and we can simply use the x,y coordinates to do our work. There could, however, be situations in which we would need to differentiate between events before acting on them. This will become clearer when we discuss how events are delivered when there are multiple components.

Our implementation of the `mouseDrag()` method does three things. First, the `messageX` and `messageY` instance variables of our class are set to the current position of the mouse. Now, having changed the coordinates for the message, we would like `HelloWeb2` to redraw itself. At first glance, it might seem logical for us to call the `paint()` method. However, you should notice that we cannot invoke `paint()` directly because we don't seem to have a `Graphics` object to pass to it. What are we to do?

We can use the `repaint()` method of the `Applet` class to request that our applet be redrawn. `repaint()` causes the Java windowing system to schedule a call to our `paint()` method at the next possible time; Java supplies the necessary `Graphics` object, as shown in Figure 5.

This mode of operation isn't just an inconvenience brought about by not having the right graphics context handy at the moment. The foremost advantage to this mode of operation is that the repainting is handled by someone else, while we are free to go about our business. The Java system has a separate, dedicated thread of execution that handles all `repaint()` requests. It can schedule and consolidate `repaint()` requests as necessary, which helps to prevent the windowing system from being overwhelmed during painting intensive situations like scrolling.

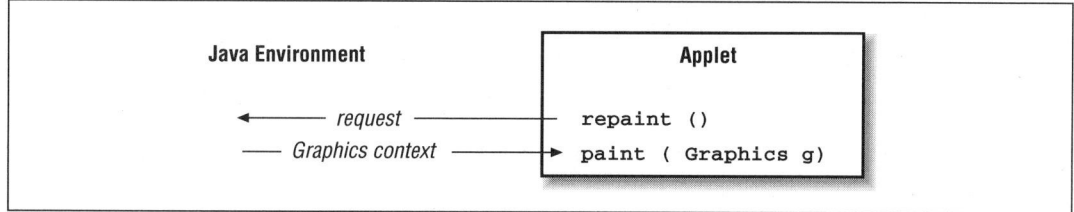

FIGURE 5: *INVOKING THE REPAINT() METHOD*

Finally, our `mouseDrag()` method returns a value to the method that called it. `mouse-Drag()` returns a Boolean value that indicates whether we have actually "handled" the event. Here we return `true`, indicating that we did indeed respond to the event and that no further processing is necessary. What would happen if we said that we had not? Well, in this example, not much. However, as we will see in the next section, certain types of components can act as containers to "hold" other components, creating a hierarchy. In this case, events that are not handled by a component are passed upward to the container component that holds it. This gives us the option of having general event handling routines that manage a number of components.

HELLO WEB! III: ATTACK OF THE BUTTON

Well, now that we have all of those concepts under control, we can move on to some fun stuff. `HelloWeb3` brings us a new graphical interface component: the `Button`. We add a `Button` component to our applet that changes the color of our text each time the button is pressed:

```
import java.applet.*;
import java.awt.*;

public class HelloWeb3 extends Applet {
        int messageX = 125, messageY = 95;
        String theMessage;
        Button theButton;
        Color[] someColors = {
                Color.black, Color.red, Color.green, Color.blue,
                Color.magenta };
        int colorIndex;

        public void init() {
                theMessage = getParameter("message");
                theButton = new Button("Change Color");
                add(theButton);
        }
```

```
public void paint( Graphics gc ) {
        gc.setColor( currentColor() );
        gc.drawString( theMessage, messageX, messageY );
}

public boolean action ( Event e, Object arg ) {
        if ( e.target == theButton ) {
                changeColor();
                return true;
        }
        return false;
}

public boolean mouseDrag(Event evt, int x, int y ) {
        messageX = x;
        messageY = y;
        repaint();
        return true;
}

synchronized private Color currentColor() {
        return someColors[ colorIndex ];
}

synchronized private void changeColor() {
        if ( ++colorIndex == someColors.length )
                colorIndex = 0;
        theButton.setForeground( currentColor() );
        repaint();
}
```

Create HelloWeb3 just as we have the other applets, and put an applet tag referencing it in an HTML document. An applet tag just like the one for HelloWeb2 will do nicely. Run the example, and you should see the display shown in Figure 6. Drag the text. Each time you press the button, the color should change. Call your friends! They should be duly impressed.

THE NEW OPERATOR

So, what have we added this time? Well, for starters we have a new variable:

```
Button theButton;
```

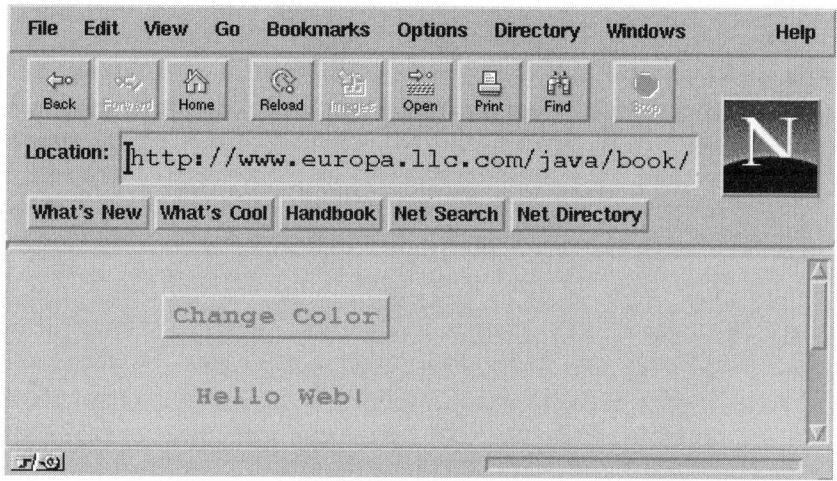

FIGURE 6: *HelloWeb! III*

The `theButton` variable is of type `Button` and is going to hold an instance of the `java.awt.Button` class. The `Button` class, as you might expect, represents a graphical button, which should look something like other buttons in your windowing system.

Two additional lines in `init()` actually create the button and cause it to be displayed in our applet:

```
theButton = new Button("Change Color");
add(theButton);
```

The first line brings us to something new. The **new** keyword is used to create an instance of a class. Recall that the variable we have declared is just an empty reference and does not yet point to a real object—in this case, an instance of the `Button` class. This is a very fundamental and important concept. We have dealt with objects previously in our examples. We have assigned them to variables, and we have called methods in them. So far, however, these objects have always been handed to us ready to go, and we have not had to explicitly create them ourselves. In the case of our `paint()` method, we were given a `Graphics` object with which to draw. The system created this instance of the `Graphics` class for our area of the screen and passed it to us in the parameter variable gc. Our `theMessage` variable is of type `String`, and we used it to hold a `String` that was returned by the `getParameter()` method. In each case, some other method instantiated (created a new instance of) the class for us.

The closest we came to actually instantiating an object was when we passed the name of the HTML **applet** parameter as an argument to the `getParameter()` method. In that case, we did cause a `String` object to be created and passed as the argument, but we did it in a somewhat sneaky fashion. As we mentioned previously, `String` objects have special status in the Java language. Because string objects are used so frequently, the Java compiler creates an instance of the **String** class for us whenever it comes across quoted text in our source code. **Strings** are, in all other respects, normal objects.

The **new** operator provides the general mechanism for instantiating objects. It is the feature of the Java language that creates a new instance of a specified class. It arranges for Java to allocate storage for the object and then calls the **constructor** method of the objects' class to initialize it.

CONSTRUCTORS

As I mentioned earlier, constructors are special methods that are called to "set up" new instances of a class. When a new object is created, Java allocates storage for it, sets variables to their default values, and then calls the constructor method for the class so that it may do whatever application-level setup is required.

A constructor method looks like a method with the same name as its class. For example, the constructor for the **Button** class is called **Button()**. Constructors do not have a return type, but, like other methods, they can take arguments. Their sole mission in life is to configure newly born class instances, possibly using whatever information was passed to them in parameters.

An object is created by calling the **new** operator with the constructor for the class and any necessary arguments. The resulting object instance is returned as a value. In our example, we create a new instance of **Button** and assign it to our **theButton** variable:

```
theButton = new Button("Change Color");
```

This **Button** constructor takes a **String** as an argument and, as it turns out, uses it to set the label of the button on the screen. A class could also, of course, provide methods that allow us to configure an object "manually" after it is created or to change its configuration at a later time. Many classes do both—the constructor simply takes its arguments and passes them to the appropriate methods. The **Button** class, for example, has a public method, **setLabel()**, that allows us to explicitly set a **Button**'s label at any time. Constructors with parameters are therefore a convenience that allows a sort of shorthand to set up a new object.

METHOD OVERLOADING

I said *this* **Button** constructor because there could be more than one. A class can have multiple, alternative constructors, each taking different parameters and possibly using them to do different kinds of set up. When there are multiple constructors for a class, Java chooses the correct one based on the types of arguments that are passed to it. We call the **Button** constructor and pass it a **String** argument, so Java locates the constructor method of the **Button** class that takes a single, **String** type argument and uses it to set up the object. This technique is called method *overloading*. All methods in Java, not just constructors, can be overloaded; this is one aspect of the object oriented programming principle of polymorphism.

A constructor method that takes no arguments is called the *default constructor*. Default constructors have a special role in the initialization of inherited class members.

COMPONENTS

We have been using the terms *component* and *container* somewhat loosely, to describe elements of an application. However, you may recall from Figure 3 that these terms are the namesakes of actual classes in the `java.awt` package.

`Component` is a base class from which all of Java's GUI components are derived. It contains variables that represent the location, shape, general appearance, and status of the object, as well as methods for basic painting and event handling. The familiar `paint()` and `mouseDrag()` methods that we have been using in our examples are actually inherited from the `Component` class. `Applet` is, of course, a kind of `Component` and inherits all of its public members just as other (perhaps simpler) types of graphical interface components do.

The `Button` class is derived from `Component` and therefore shares this same functionality. This means that the writer of the `Button` class had available methods like `paint()` and `mouseDrag()` with which to implement the behavior of the `Button` object, just as we did when creating our applet.[†] What's exciting is that we are perfectly free to further subclass components like `Button` and override their behavior to create our own special types of user interface components.

Both `Button` and `Applet` are, in this respect, equivalent. However, the `Applet` class is further derived from a class called `Container`, which gives it the added ability to "hold" other components and "manage" them.

CONTAINERS

A `Button` object is a simple user interface component. It generally makes sense only in the context of some larger application. The `Container` class is an extended type of `Component` that maintains a list of "child" components and helps to group them. The `Container` causes its children to be displayed and arranges them on the screen according to a particular scheme. A `Container` may also receive events related to its child components. As we mentioned earlier, if a component doesn't respond to a particular type of event by overriding the appropriate event handling method and handling the event, the event is passed to the parent `Container` of the component. This is the default behavior for the standard Java AWT components, which gives us a great deal of flexibility in managing interface components. We could, for example, create a "smart" button by subclassing the `Button` class and overriding certain methods to deal with the action of being pressed. Alternatively, we could simply have the `Button`'s container note which

---

† At the time of this writing, there are some limitations with respect to which events can be caught and handled by certain types of components. Not all types of components can currently intercept all types of events. The problem arises from the complications of using native windowing system GUI components in Java implementations. It is the Java development team's goal to correct this situation.

Button is pressed and handle the event appropriately. In the interest of keeping our examples contained in a single class, we use the "gestalt" view and let our Button's container, HelloWeb3, deal with its events.

Remember that Containers are Components too and, as such, can be placed alongside other Components in other Containers, in a hierarchical fashion, as shown in Figure 7. Our HelloWeb3 applet is a kind of Container and can therefore hold and manage other Java AWT components and containers like buttons, sliders, text fields, and panels.

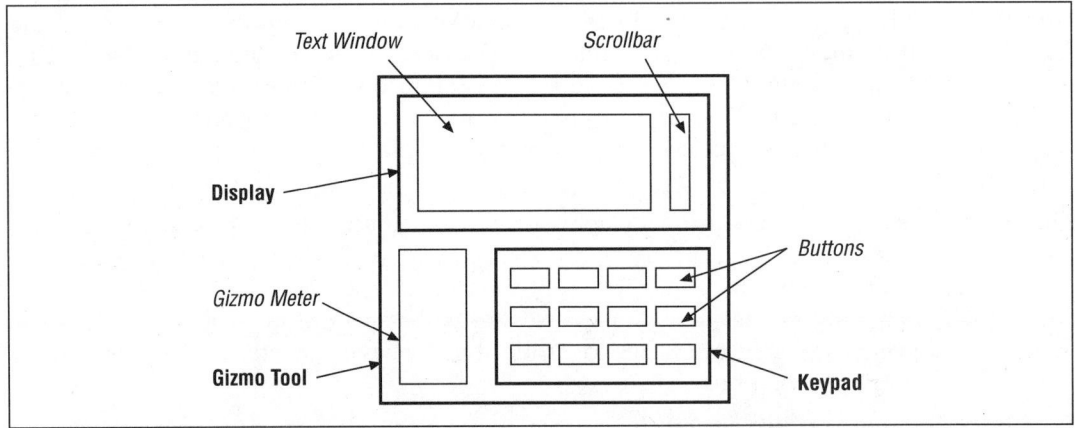

FIGURE 7: *A HYPOTHETICAL LAYOUT OF JAVA COMPONENTS AND CONTAINERS*

In Figure 7, the italicized items are Components, and the bold items are Containers. The keypad is implemented as a Container object that manages a number of keys. The keypad itself is contained in the GizmoTool container object.

LAYOUT

After creating the Button object, we would like to stick it in our applet. To do so, we invoke the add() method of Applet, passing the Button object as a parameter:

```
add(theButton);
```

add() is a method inherited by our Applet from the Container class. It appends our Button to the list of components that HelloWeb3 manages. HelloWeb3 thereafter causes the Button to be displayed, determines where on our Applet's part of the screen it should be placed, and receives events when it is pressed.

The precise location in HelloWeb3's graphics context where the Button is displayed is determined by an object called a LayoutManager. A LayoutManager class embodies a particular scheme for arranging components on the screen and adjusting their sizes. There are several standard layout managers to choose from, and we can, of course, create new ones. In our case, we use the default, and our Button should appear centered at the top of our applet.

SUBCLASSING AND SUBTYPES

If you look up the add() method of the Container class, you'll see that it takes as an argument a Component object. But in our example we're giving it a Button object. What's going on here?

Well, if you check the inheritance diagram in Figure 3 again, you'll see that Button is a subclass of the Component class. Because a subclass is a kind of its superclass and has, at minimum, all of the same public methods and variables, we can use an instance of a subclass anywhere we could use an instance of its superclass. This is another very important concept, and it is a second aspect of the object oriented principle of polymorphism. Button is a kind of Component, and any method that expects a Component as an argument accepts a Button.

ACTION( )

We have added another method to our class:

```
public boolean action ( Event e, Object arg ) {
        if ( e.target == theButton ) {
                changeColor();
                return true;
        }
        return false;
}
```

The action() method is one of the suite of event handing routines like mouseDrag(). As the name *action* might suggest however, it is a slightly more general in purpose. Components like buttons, toggle switches, and sliders cause an event to be sent whenever they are "used." These types of events are categorized as "action" events and are delivered to the action() method of the object that is to receive them. In our example, all of the action events from the "Change Color" button are passed to its container, HelloWeb3, and handled by our action() method.

In this case, there is only one Button object, and it is the only component that can cause action events. However, in a more realistic application, our applet could contain many such components, and our event handling methods would then have to make a determination as to which component was responsible for the event before acting on it. We would therefore be remiss not to take a little care and add the appropriate "check" in our action() method. (Just in case someone slips another Button into HelloWeb3 when we're not looking.)

An event contains a variable called target, which references the component that caused the event. Here we use the '==' operator in an expression to check if our Button (the one referenced by our theButton variable) is indeed that same object. If the Event that we are passed does have theButton as its target, we then call our new method changeColor() and return true, indicating that we handled this event. If the event was instigated by some other object, we do nothing and return false.

It is worth noting at this point that, in Java, the '==' operator is a test for identity and not equality. We are testing to see if `e.target` and `theButton` are the same object, not just equivalent objects.

Color Commentary

To support `HelloWeb3`'s colorful side, we have added a couple of new variables and two helpful methods. We create and initialize an array of `Color` objects representing the colors through which we cycle when our button is pressed. We also declare an integer variable that serves as an index into this array, specifying the current color:

```
Color[] someColors = {
        Color.black, Color.red, Color.green, Color.blue, Color.magenta };
int colorIndex;
```

Static Members

A number of things are going on here. First let's look at the `Color` objects that we are putting into the array. Instances of the `java.awt.Color` class represent colors and are used by all classes in the `java.awt` package that deal with color graphics.

Notice that we are referencing variables such as `Color.black` and `Color.red`. These look like normal references to an object's instance variables; however, `Color` is not an object, it is a class. What is the meaning of this?

Well, recall that in our discussion of classes and class instances, we hinted that classes can, themselves, contain methods and variables that are shared among all instances of the class. These shared members are called *static* variables and methods. The most common use for static variables of a class is to hold predefined constants or unchanging objects that all of the classes will use.

There are two advantages to this approach. First, static members can be accessed even if no instances of the class exist. A hypothetical `Component` class might have a static variable called `maximumWidth`. Some other class that has to deal with this component, such as a layout manager, might wish to know the maximum width of such a component, even if there aren't any around at the moment. Second, and more obvious, there exists only one copy of the static members, so no space is wasted to hold an extra copy of them for each class instance.

An instance of the `Color` class represents a color. For convenience, the `Color` class contains some static predefined color objects with friendly names like `green`, `red`, and (my favorite) `magenta`. An alternative to using these is to construct a color manually by specifying its RGB components in the constructor of the `Color` class. `Color.green` is thus a predefined `Color` object set to a green color. In this case, these static members of `Color` are not changeable (effectively constants); however, static variables do not, in general, have to be constant.

ARRAYS

Next, we turn our attention to the array. We have declared a variable called some-Colors, which is an array of Color objects. Arrays are syntactically supported by the Java language; however, they are true, first-class objects. This means that an array is, itself, a type of object that knows how to hold an indexed list of some other type of object. Arrays can be indexed by an integer and the resulting value is the object in the corresponding slot in the array. It is also possible to have arrays of simple numeric types; in which case, the value is also a simple numeric type.

Just as in ANSI C, when we declare an array, we can initialize it using the curly brace construct. Specifying a comma-separated list of elements inside of curly braces is a convenience that instructs the compiler to create an instance of the array with those elements and assign it to our variable. Alternatively, we could have just declared our someColors variable and, later allocated an array object for it and assigned individual elements to that array's slots.

OUR COLOR METHODS

So, we now have an array of Color objects and a variable with which to index them. What do we do with them? Well, we have declared two private methods that do the actual work for us. The private modifier on these methods specifies that they can be called only by other methods within the same instance of their class. They are not visible outside of the object. We declare members to be private to hide the detailed inner workings of a class from the outside world. This is called *encapsulation* and is another tenet of object oriented design. In this case, we have also declared our methods as private to help you recognize that they are purely our creations, to be used only by our code and distinguished from overridden methods of the Applet class.

The first method, currentColor(), is simply a convenience routine that returns the Color object representing the current text color. It returns the Color object in the some-Colors array at the index specified by our colorIndex variable:

```
synchronized private Color currentColor() {
        return someColors[ colorIndex ];
}
```

We could have just as readily used the expression someColors[colorIndex] everywhere we use currentColor(); however, creating methods to wrap common tasks is another way of shielding ourselves from the details of our class. In an alternative implementation, we might have shuffled off the details of all of the color-related code into a separate class. We could have created a class that took an array of colors in its constructor and then provided two methods: one to ask for the current color and one to cycle to the next color. (Just some food for thought).

The second method, changeColor(), is responsible for incrementing the colorIndex variable to point to the next Color in the array. changeColor() is called from our action() method whenever the button is pressed.

```
synchronized private void changeColor() {
        if ( ++colorIndex == someColors.length )
                colorIndex = 0;
        theButton.setForeground( currentColor() );
        repaint();
}
```

The syntax looks like ANSI C. We increment `colorIndex` and compare it to the length of the `someColors` array. All array objects have a variable called `length` that specifies the number of elements in the array. If we have reached the end of the array, we reset our index to zero and start over. After changing the currently selected color, we do two things. First, we call a method in our `Button` object to set the color of its label to the current color, just for consistency. Then we call `repaint()` to cause the `Applet` to be redrawn with the new color for the draggable message.

So, what is the `synchronized` keyword that appears in front of our `currentColor()` and `changeColor()` methods? Synchronization has to do with threads, which is beyond the scope of this tutorial. For now, all you need to know is that the `synchronized` keyword indicates that these two methods can never run at the same time. They must always run one after the other. The reason is that in `changeColor()` we increment `colorIndex` before testing its value. That means that for some very brief period of time while Java is running through our code, `colorIndex` can have a value that is "past the end" of our array. If our `currentColor()` method could happen to run at that same moment, we would see a run-time "array out of bounds" error. If you go on to learn more about Java, you'll see that the language makes dealing with these kinds of problems easy through language-level synchronization support.

Finally, our `paint()` method has been modified to set the current color in its `Graphics` object before doing any drawing:

```
public void paint( Graphics gc ) {
        gc.setColor( currentColor() );
        gc.drawString( theMessage, messageX, messageY );
}
```

Subsequent drawing calls on this `Graphics` object, like the one we make to `drawString()`, render in that color. We must set the color from our `paint()` method because we are handed a new *Graphics* object on each invocation—a "blank slate," if you will. We are responsible for remembering everything about how we draw our applet's face. In contrast, you should recall that our `Button` object has it's own `paint()` method and is therefore responsible for remembering its own appearance, including its current color. That is why we can safely set that property for the `Button` once, right in the `changeColor()` method.

Well, we will now say goodbye to HelloWeb. I hope this tutorial has helped you develop a feel for the major features of the Java language and that you will continue to explore Java on your own. There are many exciting applications to come and it will be interesting to see how Java changes the face of the Web.

THE X SYNCHRONIZATION EXTENSION

Martha Zimet

ABSTRACT

Development of the X Synchronization Extension has been motivated by multi-media applications. While these applications perform adequately in some environments, this is not the case in a distributed environment such as X, in which unpredictable operating systems and network delays can occur. The core X protocol does not guarantee the relative order or the timing of request execution on the client's behalf.

Under the Synchronization Extension, applications on the same host, or on different hosts running different operating systems, can be synchronized. The extension uses a mechanism whereby the X server internally determines when requests are executed. This mechanism can be used by a variety of applications that require synchronization, including programs that need synchronized audio, video, and graphics data; animation programs that require images displayed at regular intervals; overlay drawing applications; clock and timer applications; and screen savers.

This article describes version 3.0 of the X Synchronization Extension, which is an X Consortium standard [Glauert94]. It explains the purpose, concepts, and interface of the X Synchronization Extension and provides an example of how to use it. At the end of the article are reference pages for the C language binding to the extension protocol and the procedures that manipulate 64-bit values.

Martha Zimet (zimet@manray.com) is a software consultant specializing in the X Window System. She has previously held positions as a software quality architect at Network Computing Devices and a staff engineer at SunSoft. Martha is also the architect of the RECORD extension.

INTRODUCTION

The core X11 protocol does not make any absolute guarantees about the time at which client requests are executed or the order of their execution. These constraints are not problematic for most clients. However, due to unpredictable network and operating system delays, they are problematic for clients that need to synchronize with each other, display images or graphics at regular intervals or in batches, or synchronize multiple data streams such as audio and video. The X Synchronization Extension provides facilities that address these issues. The X Synchronization Extension is implemented in both code extensions to the X server and in the extension client library *libXext*; the server extension is known as SYNC, and the client library functions are known collectively as XSync.

The Synchronization Extension allows two or more clients to determine the relative order in which their requests are executed by the X server, without having to coordinate their requests directly with each other in an operating system or network-dependent manner. The extension also allows a single client to delay its requests until a given X server time is reached or until some other change occurs. In addition, the extension allows clients to receive regular event notification when certain changes occur within the X server. Finally, the extension allows a simple priority to be given to each client.

Using XSync, an animation application that displays images at regular intervals could send any number of animation frames to the X server as a single unit. The X server would then interpret the synchronization requests between frames and play the animation at the correct speed. This provides the benefits of request batching and low latency.

The Synchronization Extension does not, however, provide true real-time behavior since the server cannot interrupt one request in order to execute another request. In addition, the extension does not guarantee request execution times, although clients can request notification when a specific deadline has been missed.

This article begins by providing an overview of extension concepts and terminology. Then it describes the XSync API functions and utility procedures, followed by short code examples using XSync. The article concludes with some complete programs that use XSync.

EXTENSION CONCEPTS

In order to understand how the Synchronization Extension works, you must be familiar with the following extension-specific terminology: counter, trigger, wait condition, alarm, and priority.

COUNTERS

A *counter* is the internal extension object on which clients synchronize. XSync defines `XSyncCounter` as a counter type. The two types of counters, system counters and client counters, are used by clients in the following ways:

- The client blocks until a counter reaches a certain value (called a *wait condition*).
- The client receives an event when a counter reaches a certain value (called an *alarm*).

All X servers that implement the Synchronization Extension are required to provide a system counter called SERVERTIME that increments in milliseconds from an arbitrary starting point. Some X servers also provide FRAMEEND, which advances by one when the display hardware completes the display of a new frame. All system counters are updated by the server only, not by clients, and while the current value of a system counter can be queried by clients, system counters cannot be destroyed by clients.

Client counters, on the other hand, can be created and initialized by clients. Client counters can also be queried by clients, destroyed by clients, and updated by clients. The code to create and use a client counter would look something like the following:

```
Display *dpy;
XSyncValue create_value, delta_value, read_value;
Bool overflow;
XSyncCounter counter;

XSyncIntToValue(&create_value, 0);
counter = XSyncCreateCounter(dpy, create_value);
XSyncIntToValue(&delta_value, 10);
XSyncChangeCounter(dpy, counter, delta_value);
XSyncQueryCounter(dpy, counter, &read_value);
```

In this code example, the procedure XSyncIntToValue() is used to convert an integer value to a 64-bit value, which is then used as the counter's initial value. The client counter is created with the XSyncCreateCounter() request. XSyncIntToValue() is again used to convert an integer value to a 64-bit value, this time to update the counter value. The code updates the counter value with the XSyncChangeCounter() request and then queries the counter with XSyncQueryCounter().

TRIGGERS

A *trigger* defines a test on a counter and has a value of either True or False. The value of the test is determined by the combination of the trigger parameter values, which include a counter, a wait value, a wait type, and a test type. The importance of triggers is that they are used by clients when specifying both wait conditions and alarms.

The trigger structure is defined as follows:

```
typedef struct {
    XSyncCounter counter;
    XSyncValueType value_type;
    XSyncValue wait_value;
    XSyncTestType test_type;
} XSyncTrigger;
```

The counter field is either a client counter or a system counter. wait_value is the counter value the trigger is waiting for, while value_type specifies whether the value is absolute or relative. When value_type is absolute, the test value is simply wait_value. When value_type is relative, the test value is the value of the counter plus `wait_value`. `test_type` indicates the type of test that is performed, which controls whether the trigger is `True` or `False`. The possible values of `test_type` and the conditions under which the trigger test value is `True` are:

`XSyncPositiveTransition`

> Trigger test value is `True` when the counter changes from a value less than the test value to a value greater than or equal to the test value.

`XSyncNegativeTransition`

> Trigger test value is `True` when the counter changes from a value greater than the test value to a value less than or equal to the test value.

`XSyncPositiveComparison`

> Trigger test value is `True` when the counter is greater than or equal to the test value.

`XSyncNegativeComparison`

> Trigger test value is `True` when the counter is less than or equal to the test value.

If a client tries to use a trigger on an invalid counter, a `BadCounter` error results.

WAIT CONDITIONS

A *wait condition* is used as a parameter in the `XSyncAwait()` request that a client uses to block until the trigger in the wait condition is `True`. The wait condition also includes a value, known as an event threshold, that determines if an `XSyncCounterNotify` event is generated when the client unblocks. Whether or not the event is generated is determined by subtracting the test value from the counter value. For positive `test_type` conditions (`XSyncPositiveTransition`, `XSyncPositiveComparison`), an event is generated when the difference is greater than or equal to the event threshold. For negative `test_type` conditions (`XSyncNegativeTransition`, `XSyncNegativeComparison`), an event is generated when the difference is less than or equal to the event threshold.

The wait condition structure is as follows:

```
typedef struct {
    XSyncTrigger trigger;
    XSyncValue event_threshold;
} XSyncWaitCondition;
```

When a client issues the `XSyncAwait()` request, it specifies the particular wait conditions (trigger and event threshold). The request blocks until the counter reaches some value as specified in the wait condition. When that value is reached, the client is unblocked, and request processing continues. The code to do this would look something like the following:

```
/* Counter is defined elsewhere. */
XSyncCounter counter;
static XSyncWaitCondition cond;
XSyncValue sync_delay;
```

```
XSyncValue sync_count;
Bool overflow;

/* Retrieve counter initial value. */
XSyncQueryCounter(dpy, counter, &sync_count);

/* Add update to initial counter value.*/
XSyncValueAdd(&sync_count, sync_count, sync_delay, &overflow);

/* Set wait condition trigger. */
cond.trigger.wait_value = sync_count;
cond.trigger.counter = server_time;
cond.trigger.value_type = XSyncAbsolute;
cond.trigger.test_type = XSyncPositiveComparison;

/* Set wait condition event threshold to 1. */
XSyncIntToValue(&cond.event_threshold, 1);

/* Block until trigger is True. */
XSyncAwait(dpy, &cond, 1);
```

In this code example, `XSyncQueryCounter()` is used to obtain the current value of a counter. Then `XSyncValueAdd()` is used to set the trigger `wait_value` by adding a delay value to the current counter value, both of which are 64-bit values. The other wait condition parameters are then set, including the event threshold, which is set by converting the integer value 1 to a 64-bit value with `XSyncIntToValue()`. Finally, the `XSyncAwait()` request is issued.

ALARMS

Clients use *alarms* to receive notification via an `XSyncAlarmNotify` event when a counter reaches a certain value. XSync defines `XSyncAlarm` as an alarm type. The advantages of using alarms over `XSyncAwait()` requests are that the client is not blocked, multiple clients can share an alarm, and one request can result in multiple events.

A trigger is associated with an alarm when it is created with the `XSyncCreateAlarm()` request or modified via the `XSyncChangeAlarm()` request. If a client attempts to perform an operation on an invalid alarm, a `BadAlarm` error results. When the trigger becomes `True`, the alarm goes off, and an `XSyncAlarmNotify` event is generated and delivered to all interested clients. After the alarm goes off, the alarm trigger is automatically updated by a value known as the delta value. This value is specified by the client when the alarm is created or modified. The client also specifies whether or not it wishes to receive an `XSyncAlarmNotify` event.

When an alarm is created or modified, values contained in an `XSyncAlarmAttributes` structure are used in combination with a mask. The structure is defined as follows:

```
typedef struct {
    XSyncTrigger trigger;
    XSyncValue  delta;
    Bool events;
    XSyncAlarmState state;
} XSyncAlarmAttributes;
```

The relationship between field values and mask values are shown in Table 1.

FIELD NAME	ALARM MASK
trigger.counter	XSyncACounter
trigger.value_type	XSyncAValueType
trigger.wait_value	XSyncAValue
trigger.test_type	XSyncATestType
delta	XSyncADelta
events	XSyncAEvents
state	cannot be set by client

TABLE 1: *FIELDS AND MASKS*

The code to create an alarm would look something like the following:

```
XSyncCounter counter;        /* Counter is assigned elsewhere. */
XSyncAlarm alarm = None;
XSyncValue sync_delay;       /* Delta amount; assigned elsewhere. */
XSyncAlarmAttributes alarm_values;
unsigned long alarm_mask;

/* Trigger test value is counter value + wait_value. */
alarm_values.trigger.counter = counter;
alarm_values.trigger.value_type = XSyncRelative;
alarm_values.trigger.wait_value = sync_delay;
alarm_values.trigger.test_type = XSyncPositiveComparison;
alarm_values.delta = sync_delay;
alarm_values.events = True;
alarm_mask = XSyncCACounter | XSyncCAValueType |
    XSyncCAValue | XSyncCATestType | XSyncCADelta | XSyncCAEvents;
alarm = XSyncCreateAlarm(dpy, alarm_mask, alarm_values);
```

PRIORITIES

The synchronization extension provides a scheduling priority mechanism. With this mechanism, the X protocol requests of higher priority clients are executed by the X server before those of lower priority clients. The importance of scheduling priority is that it can improve animation smoothness on X servers with a high load.

XSYNC API

The XSync API consists of 15 functions that are declared in the header file *X11/extensions/ sync.h*. This header file must be included in all programs that use XSync. The functions themselves are included in the library *libXext*. The XSync functions are listed below; the routines are fully described in the reference pages at the end of this article.

Initialization

- XSyncQueryExtension() determines if the extension is supported.
- XSyncInitialize() determines the supported protocol version.
- XSyncListSystemCounters() returns a list of supported system counters.
- XSyncFreeSystemCounterList() frees the list returned by XSyncListSystem-Counters().

Counter Requests

- XSyncCreateCounter() creates a client counter.
- XSyncQueryCounter() queries a counter value.
- XSyncSetCounter() sets the value of a client counter.
- XSyncChangeCounter() adds a value to a client counter.
- XSyncDestroyCounter() destroys a client counter.

Await Request

- XSyncAwait() sets up a wait condition.

Alarm Requests

- XSyncCreateAlarm() creates an alarm.
- XSyncQueryAlarm() queries alarm attributes.
- XSyncChangeAlarm() changes alarm attributes.
- XSyncDestroyAlarm() destroys an alarm.

Priority Requests

- XSyncSetPriority() sets a client's priority.
- XSyncGetPriority() gets a client's priority.

Since counter, trigger, and wait condition parameters require 64-bit values, utility procedures are provided as part of the XSync interface to convert integer values to 64-bit values, compare 64-bit values, and perform arithmetic operations on 64-bit values. These procedures are client-side operations; they send no protocol request. Each 64-bit value is composed of a low 32-bit value and a high 32-bit value. The 64-bit value type is XSyncValue. These routines are listed below and described in the reference section at the end of this article.

Conversion Procedures

- XSyncIntToValue()
- XSyncIntstoValue()

Comparison Procedures

- XSyncValueGreaterThan()
- XSyncValueLessThan()
- XSyncValueGreaterThanOrEqual()
- XSyncValueEqual()

Sign Procedures

- XSyncValueIsNegative()
- XSyncValueIsZero()
- XSyncVaueIsPositive()

Low/High Procedures

- XSyncValueLow32()
- XSyncValueHigh32()

Arithmetic Procedures

- XSyncValueAdd()
- XSyncValueSubtract()

Min/Max Procedures

- XSyncMaxValue()
- XSyncMinValue()

USING XSYNC

Since graphics programs most readily show the usage of the Synchronization Extension, the examples in this section are simple rendering programs. Regardless of the application, three basic steps are required by XSync applications:

- Initialize the extension by determining whether SYNC is available on the display and establishing which protocol version is supported and what system counters are available.

- Establish the synchronization trigger for a wait condition or an alarm.

- Set up a loop that alternates between generating a single frame of graphics and testing whether the trigger is `True`.

EXTENSION INITIALIZATION

The function `XSyncQueryExtension()` tells you whether SYNC is available on a server. The code usually looks like this:

```
Display *dpy;
int sync_event, sync_error;
if(!XSyncQueryExtension(dpy, &sync_event, &sync_error)
{
    fprintf( stderr,
        "%s:  SYNC extension not supported on server \"%s\"\n",
        ProgramName, DisplayString( dpy ) );
    XCloseDisplay( dpy );
    exit(1);
}
```

`XSyncQueryExtension()` returns `True` (nonzero) if the SYNC extension exists on the specified display. The values returned in `sync_event` and `sync_error` are used to form the extension event types and error codes by adding them to constants (such as `XSyncCounterNotify` and `BadCounter`) defined in *X11/extensions/sync.h*.

A client must initialize the extension before using it and does this only once through `XSyncInitialize()`, which returns the protocol version number supported in the server. `XSyncQueryExtension()` is the only XSync function that the client can call before `XSyncInitialize()`.

The complete programs at the end of this article use the `SERVERTIME` system counter instead of creating their own client counters. Therefore, verifying the availability of `SERVERTIME` through `XSyncListSystemCounters()` is part of the initialization process. The following function `DoSyncInit()` is a complete initialization procedure, which returns `True` or `False`. This function is used in both of the complete programs at the end of this section. If `False` is returned, the initialization has failed, and the program can exit gracefully.

```
int sync_major, sync_minor;
int sync_event, sync_error;
int AlarmNotify, CounterNotify;
XSyncCounter server_time = None;
char *ServerTimerName = NULL;
```

```
Bool
DoSyncInit(dpy)
Display *dpy;
{
    int n_counters, i;
    XSyncSystemCounter *sys_counter_list = NULL;

    /* Verify SYNC is available on the display. */
    if(!XSyncQueryExtension(dpy, &sync_event, &sync_error))
    {
        fprintf( stderr,
            "%s:  SYNC extension not supported on server \"%s\"\n",
            ProgramName, DisplayString( dpy ) );
        return(False);
    }

    /* Initialize and verify SYNC protocol version. */
    if (!XSyncInitialize(dpy, &sync_major, &sync_minor))
    {
        fprintf( stderr,
            "%s:  Cannot initialize SYNC extension on server \"%s\"\n",
            ProgramName, DisplayString( dpy ) );
        return(False);
    }
    else
    {
        /* If SYNC and XSync versions are different.. */
        if (sync_major != SYNC_MAJOR_VERSION ||
            sync_minor != SYNC_MINOR_VERSION)
        {
            fprintf(stderr,
                "Warning: Program: %d.%2.2d, Server: %d.%2.2d\n",
                sync_major, sync_minor,
                SYNC_MAJOR_VERSION, SYNC_MAJOR_VERSION);
        }
    }

    /* Form events from returned event base. */
    AlarmNotify = sync_event + XSyncAlarmNotify;
    CounterNotify = sync_event + XSyncCounterNotify;

    /* Verify SERVERTIME system counter is available. */
    sys_counter_list = XSyncListSystemCounters(dpy, &n_counters);
    for (i = n_counters-1; i >= 0; i--)
```

```
        {
            if (strcmp(sys_counter_list[i].name, "SERVERTIME")==0)
            {
                server_time = sys_counter_list[i].counter;
                ServerTimerName = sys_counter_list[i].name;
                break;
            }
        }

        /* Free system counter list. */
        XSyncFreeSystemCounterList(sys_counter_list);
        if(server_time == None)
            return(False);

        return(True);
    }
```

The function performs the following actions:

1. Calls **XSyncQueryExtension()** to verify that the SYNC extension is available on the specified X server.

2. Calls **XSyncInitialize()** to initialize the extension and verify that the XSync library protocol version is compatible with the X server SYNC protocol version.

3. Adds the value returned in **sync_event** to constants to form event types that can be used with **XNextEvent()** or other event queue processing requests.

4. Determines whether or not **SERVERTIME** is available using the **XSyncListSystem-Counters()** request, which returns a list of available system counters.

5. Assigns the value of **SERVERTIME** to the variable **server_time**, which is an **XSyncCounter**.

6. Frees the list of counters with the **XSyncFreeSystemCounterList()** request.

ESTABLISHING A WAIT CONDITION AND ALARM TRIGGERS

After a client initializes the SYNC extension, it needs to specify triggers that can be used with either wait conditions (**XSyncAwait**) or alarms (**XSyncCreateAlarm**). As explained earlier, a trigger defines a test condition for either a client counter or a system counter.

WAIT CONDITION

The following example shows the creation of a trigger for a wait condition. Since the trigger **value_type** is **XSyncAbsolute**, the trigger test value is simply **wait_value**. The example uses the counter **server_time**, which is an **XSyncCounter** type that was assigned to the system counter **SERVERTIME** in the **DoSyncInit()** example. A system counter is used instead of a client counter since system counters are updated automatically by the server and do not need to be updated by the client.

```
/* wait value update */
int global_delay = 25;
static XSyncWaitCondition cond = None;
XSyncValue sync_delay;
XSyncValue sync_count;

/* Convert integer to 64 bit value. */
XSyncIntToValue(&sync_delay, global_delay);

/* Retrieve system counter initial value. */
XSyncQueryCounter(dpy, server_time, &sync_count);

/* Add update to initial counter value.*/
XSyncValueAdd(&sync_count, sync_count, sync_delay, &overflow);

/* Set wait conditions. */
cond.trigger.counter = server_time;
cond.trigger.value_type = XSyncAbsolute;
cond.trigger.test_type = XSyncPositiveComparison;

/* Set event threshold to 1 to show any missed deadlines. */
XSyncIntToValue(&cond.event_threshold, 1);
```

You may have noticed that the code does not set the trigger's `wait_value`, which is because `wait_value` is updated continuously in the loop described in the next section. The code does set the update amount, however, using the variable `sync_delay`. The code also obtains the initial value of the counter `server_time`, using the `XSyncQueryCounter()` request. The update value is then added to the initial value of `server_time` with the procedure `XSyncValueAdd()`.

ALARM

An alarm initialization is shown in the following example. The alarm sends frames of graphics in batches. Since the trigger `value_type` is `XSyncRelative`, the trigger test value is the value of the counter added to `wait_value`. The counter `server_time`, an `XSyncCounter` that was previously assigned to the system counter SERVERTIME, is used again.

```
static XSyncAlarm server_alarm = None;
int global_delay = 25;
int global_batch = 2;
int status;
XSyncValue sync_delay;
XSyncValue sync_count;
```

```
XSyncAlarmAttributes alarm_values;
unsigned long alarm_mask;

/* Calculate alarm delta as delay * frames in batch. */
XSyncIntToValue(&sync_delay, global_delay*global_batch);

/* Trigger test value is counter value + wait_value. */
alarm_values.trigger.counter = server_time;
alarm_values.trigger.value_type = XSyncRelative;
alarm_values.trigger.wait_value = sync_delay;
alarm_values.trigger.test_type = XSyncPositiveComparison;
alarm_values.delta = sync_delay;
alarm_values.events = True;
alarm_mask = XSyncCACounter | XSyncCAValueType |
    XSyncCAValue | XSyncCATestType | XSyncCADelta | XSyncCAEvents;

server_alarm = XSyncCreateAlarm(dpy, alarm_mask, alarm_values);
```

After each `XSyncAlarmNotify` event in the loop in the next section, the alarm updates automatically by adding its `delta` value to the trigger `wait_value`. Since the alarm sends a number of frames in a single batch, the delay value is multiplied by the number of frames in a batch to calculate `delta`. This value is also used as the initial `wait_value` in order to start synchronization with the first batch of frames.

SYNCHRONIZATION LOOP

The third step in the synchronization process is the most complicated. If any events are pending, this loop needs to process the event queue. Essentially, the loop waits for a synchronization event and when it occurs it performs some graphics rendering. With a wait condition, the synchronization event is a trigger being `True`, while with an alarm it's an `XSyncAlarmNotify` event.

WAIT CONDITION

With a wait condition, the loop updates the trigger `wait_value` and blocks until the trigger is `True`. Then the loop can calculate and render the next frame of graphics. The following code shows these actions; this code is used in the complete programs in the following section.

```
Bool overflow;

/* Update wait value. */
XSyncValueAdd(&sync_count, sync_count, sync_delay, &overflow);
cond.trigger.wait_value = sync_count;

/* Block until trigger is True. */
```

```
XSyncAwait(dpy, &cond, 1);

/* Calculate and render graphics. */
DoReDraw(False);
```

ALARM

With an alarm, the loop waits until the next XSyncAlarmNotify event occurs. When it does, the loop calculates the number of frames to send and then calculates and renders that next batch of graphics frames. The following example shows these actions, which are used in the first program in the following section. The predicate procedure, `Predic-cateProc()`, is used with `XIfEvent()` to check the event queue for an `XSyncAlarm-Notify` event. The number of frames to send is calculated based on the current counter value, the current alarm value, and the batch size specified on the command line. This allows the program to catch up if the rendering operations fall behind the drawing operations.

```
Bool
PredicateProc(dpy, xev, arg)
Display  *dpy;
XEvent *xev;
char *arg;
{
    /* Return value is tested in XIfEvent() */
    if(xev->type == AlarmNotify)
        return True;
    else
        return False;
}


XEvent xev;
XSyncAlarmNotifyEvent *pane;
char *stuff = (char *)NULL;
XSyncValue to_do;
Bool overflow;

/* Alarm updates automatically: delta is added to wait_value. */
XIfEvent(dpy, &xev, PredicateProc, stuff);

pane = (XSyncAlarmNotifyEvent *)&xev;

/* Determine if request batch needs to catch up. */
XSyncValueSubtract(&to_do, pane->counter_value,
    pane->alarm_value, &overflow);
frames_to_do += global_batch +
    XSyncValueLow32(to_do)/XSyncValueLow32(sync_delay);
```

```
    /* Send next block of requests. */
    while(frames_to_do)
    {
        DoReDraw(False);
        frames_to_do--;
    }
```

COMPLETE XSYNC PROGRAMS

The concepts described previously are used in complete examples in this section. The first complete program uses only Xlib to illustrate XSync synchronization based on a wait condition or an alarm, which is selectable by command-line options. The second complete program uses Motif and the X Toolkit; it also illustrates synchronization based on a wait condition or an alarm. Both programs have a command-line option that specifies the number of frames that are batched together when an alarm is used. Sending the protocol requests to draw a number of frames in a single batch makes the data transport to the server more efficient and can be used in complex graphics rendering programs where the rendering takes place in the background.

WINDOW PROGRAM

The first program *syncit* uses Xlib to illustrate synchronization. This program allows command-line selection of a wait condition or alarm synchronization (wait condition is the default). A delay amount, used by both the wait condition and the alarm, can also be specified on the command line. When the delay is not specified, no synchronization takes place. Without synchronization, the graphics update is too fast, as evidenced by the image flicker, and the animation does not catch up when the window is moved, mapped, or resized. With synchronization, the animation drawing is consistent, flicker is reduced, and the animation catches up if necessary. Delay amounts greater than 25 milliseconds are most useful to show the difference between animation with and without synchronization. The number of frames to be batched, which is used only by the alarm, can also be specified on the command line.

Here are some usage examples. If you don't want to use a wait condition or an alarm, type the following:

```
% syncit -display manray:0
```

To use a wait condition with a delay of 25 milliseconds:

```
% syncit -display manray:0 -delay 25
```

To use an alarm with a delay of 25 milliseconds and batch size of 2:

```
% syncit -display manray:0 -delay 25 -batch 2 -alarm
```

The *syncit* program uses the `DoSyncInit()` function shown earlier. During execution, the program performs the following operations:

- Processes the command-line options.
- Opens a connection to the display.
- If a delay is specified, initializes the SYNC extension.
- Creates a window and the XOR drawing graphics context.
- If a delay is specified, initializes a wait condition or an alarm and loops through the animation using the wait condition or the alarm.
- If no delay is specified, loops through the animation.

```c
#ifndef lint
static char sccsid[ ] = "@(#) syncit.c 1.8 2/20/95";
#endif

#include <stdio.h>
#include <math.h>

#include <X11/Xlib.h>
#include <X11/Xutil.h>
#include <X11/Xos.h>
#include <X11/Xatom.h>
#include <X11/extensions/sync.h>

#define POINTS 6

static Display *dpy;
static int screen;
static Colormap cmap;
static Window win;
static XEvent xev;
static  GC star_xor_gc;

Atom protocol_atom, wm_delete_atom;
XClientMessageEvent *cme;
char *ProgramName = "unknown_program";
Bool init = True;
Bool blocking = False;
Bool use_sync = False;
Bool use_wait = True;
Bool use_alarm = False;

double start_angle;
int width, height;
```

```c
XPoint prev_points[POINTS];
XPoint points[POINTS];
long star, bg;

/* Sync Stuff */
static XSyncCounter server_time = None;
static XSyncAlarm    server_alarm = None;
static XSyncWaitCondition cond = None;

static int global_batch = 1;
static int global_delay = 0;
static int frames_to_do = 0;
static int AlarmNotify = 0;
static int CounterNotify = 0;

XSyncValue sync_delay;
XSyncValue sync_count;
int sync_major, sync_minor;
int sync_event, sync_error;

/* Forward declarations */
void DoRotate();
Bool DoSyncInit();
void ExpectAlarmNotify();
Bool PredicateProc();
void ChangeAlarm();
void DoReDraw();

static void Usage ()
{
    static char *help[] = {
"    -help                print this message",
"    -display displayname  X server to contact",
"    -delay #             amount to delay",
"    -batch #             number of frames to batch (default is 1)",
"    -alarm               use alarm for delay",
"    -wait                use wait condition for delay (default)",
"", NULL };
    char **cpp;
    fprintf (stderr, "Usage:         %s [-options ...]\n\n",
             ProgramName);
    fprintf (stderr, "where options include:\n");
    for (cpp = help; *cpp; cpp++) {
        fprintf (stderr, "%s\n", *cpp);
```

```
        }
        exit (1);
}


main(argc, argv)
int argc;
char *argv[];
{
    char *displayname = NULL;
    XWindowAttributes  xwa;
    register int i;

    ProgramName = argv[0];

    /* Process command line arguments: */
    for (i = 1; i < argc; i++) {
        if (!strcmp(argv[i], "-help")) {
            Usage();
        }
        if(!strcmp(argv[i], "-display")){
            if (++i >= argc)
                Usage();
            displayname = argv[i];
            continue;
        }
        if(!strcmp(argv[i], "-delay")) {
            if (++i >= argc)
                Usage();
            global_delay = atoi(argv[i]);
            use_sync = True;
            continue;
        }
        if(!strcmp(argv[i], "-batch")) {
            if (++i >= argc)
                Usage();
            global_batch = atoi(argv[i]);
            use_sync = True;
            continue;
        }
        if(!strcmp(argv[i], "-alarm")) {
            use_alarm = True;
            use_wait = False;
            continue;
        }
```

```c
        if(!strcmp(argv[i], "-wait")) {
            use_alarm = False;
            use_wait = True;
            continue;
        }

        Usage();
    }
    if (!(dpy= XOpenDisplay(displayname)))
    {
        fprintf(stderr, "Cannot open display: %s\n", displayname);
        exit(-1);
    }
    screen = DefaultScreen(dpy);
    star = WhitePixel(dpy, screen);
    bg = BlackPixel(dpy, screen);

    CreateWindow();

    XMapWindow(dpy, win);
    XFlush(dpy);

    while (1)
    {
        XNextEvent(dpy, &xev);
        if (xev.type == Expose)
            break;
    }

    XGetWindowAttributes(dpy, win, &xwa);
    width = xwa.width / 2;
    height = xwa.height / 2;
    start_angle = 0.0;

    if (use_sync)
    {
        if(!DoSyncInit(dpy))
        {
            XCloseDisplay(dpy);
            exit(1);
        }

        /* Convert delay to 64 bit value for wait and alarm.
        XSyncIntToValue(&sync_delay, global_delay); */
```

```
    /* Synchronization trigger for XSyncAwait(). */
    if(use_wait)
    {
        Bool overflow;

        /* Convert delay to 64 bit value. */
        XSyncIntToValue(&sync_delay, global_delay);

        /* Retrieve system counter initial value. */
        XSyncQueryCounter(dpy, server_time, &sync_count);
        fprintf(stderr, "%s  (initial value: %d)\n",
            "SERVERTIME", XSyncValueLow32(sync_count));

         /* Add delay to counter value.*/
        XSyncValueAdd(&sync_count, sync_count, sync_delay, &overflow);

        /* Set wait conditions. */
        cond.trigger.counter = server_time;
        cond.trigger.value_type = XSyncAbsolute;
        cond.trigger.test_type = XSyncPositiveComparison;

        /* Set event threshold to 1 to show any missed deadlines. */
        XSyncIntToValue(&cond.event_threshold, 1);
    }

    /* Synchronization trigger for XSyncAlarmNotify. */
    if(use_alarm)
    {
        server_alarm = XSyncCreateAlarm(dpy,
            0L, (XSyncAlarmAttributes *)NULL);

        /* Calculate alarm delta as delay * frames in batch. */
        XSyncIntToValue(&sync_delay, global_delay*global_batch);

        /* Trigger test value is counter value + wait_value. */
        ChangeAlarm(dpy, server_alarm, server_time, XSyncRelative,
            /* wait_value */ sync_delay, XSyncPositiveComparison,
            /* delta      */ sync_delay, True);
    }
}

while(1)  /* Loop */
{
```

```
        if (blocking || XPending(dpy))
        {
            XNextEvent(dpy, &xev);
            switch (xev.type)
            {
                case ClientMessage:
                    cme = (XClientMessageEvent *)&xev;
                    if (cme->message_type == protocol_atom
                        && cme->data.l[0] == wm_delete_atom)
                        {
                            if(use_alarm)
                                XSyncDestroyAlarm(dpy, server_alarm);
                            XCloseDisplay(dpy);
                            exit(1);
                        }
                    break;
                case MapNotify:
                    blocking = False;
                    break;
                case UnmapNotify:
                    blocking = True;
                    continue;
                case Expose:
                    DoReDraw(True);
                    blocking = False;
                    break;
                case VisibilityNotify:
                case ResizeRequest:
                    blocking = False;
                    break;
                case ConfigureNotify:
                    width = xev.xconfigure.width/2;
                    height = xev.xconfigure.height/2;
                    DoReDraw(True);
                    blocking = False;
                    break;
                default:
                    break;
            }
        }

        if(use_sync)
            DoRotate();
        else
```

```
                DoReDraw(False);

        } /* End loop */
}


void
DoReDraw(winev)
Bool  winev;
{
    register int i;
    double angle;

    if(!init)
    {
        if(winev)
            XClearWindow(dpy, win);
        else
            XDrawLines(dpy, win, star_xor_gc,
                prev_points, POINTS, CoordModeOrigin);
    }
    start_angle += M_PI / 60.0;
    angle = start_angle;
    for (i=0; i<POINTS; i++)
    {
        points[i].x = width + width * cos(angle);
        points[i].y = height + height * sin(angle);
        prev_points[i].x = points[i].x;
        prev_points[i].y = points[i].y;
        angle += 4.0 * M_PI / ((double) (POINTS-1));
    }
    if(init)
        init = False;

    XDrawLines(dpy, win, star_xor_gc,
        points, POINTS, CoordModeOrigin);
}


CreateWindow()
{
    XSetWindowAttributes xswa;
    XGCValues val;
    unsigned long value_mask = 0;

    xswa.background_pixel = BlackPixel(dpy, screen);
```

```
        xswa.border_pixel = BlackPixel(dpy, screen);
        xswa.colormap = cmap;
        xswa.event_mask = ExposureMask | VisibilityChangeMask |
            StructureNotifyMask;

        value_mask |= CWColormap | CWBackPixel | CWBorderPixel;

        win = XCreateWindow(dpy, RootWindow(dpy, screen),
            400, 400, 100, 100, 0, DefaultDepth(dpy, screen),
            InputOutput, DefaultVisual(dpy, screen), value_mask, &xswa);

        /* Set up star GXxor graphics context. */
        val.foreground = star;
        val.background = bg;
        val.foreground = val.foreground ^ val.background ;
        val.function = GXxor ;

        star_xor_gc = XCreateGC(dpy, win,
            GCForeground | GCBackground | GCFunction, &val);

        XChangeProperty(dpy, win, XA_WM_NAME, XA_STRING, 8,
            PropModeReplace, (unsigned char *)"Sync", 4);

        protocol_atom = XInternAtom(dpy, "WM_PROTOCOLS", False);
        wm_delete_atom = XInternAtom(dpy, "WM_DELETE_WINDOW", False);
        XSetWMProtocols(dpy, win, &wm_delete_atom, 1);

        XSelectInput(dpy, win, StructureNotifyMask | ExposureMask |
            VisibilityChangeMask);
    }

void
DoRotate()
{
    if(use_wait)
    {
        Bool overflow;

        XSync(dpy, False);

        /* Update wait value. */
        XSyncValueAdd(&sync_count, sync_count, sync_delay, &overflow);
        cond.trigger.wait_value = sync_count;
```

```
        /* Block until trigger is True. */
        XSyncAwait(dpy, &cond, 1);

        /* Calculate and render graphics. */
        DoReDraw(False);
    }
    if(use_alarm)
        ExpectAlarmNotify(dpy);

    return;
}


void
ChangeAlarm(dpy, alarm, counter, valtype, testval, testtype, delta, events)
Display *dpy;
XSyncAlarm alarm;
XSyncCounter counter;
XSyncValue  testval, delta;
int valtype, testtype, events;
{
    XSyncAlarmAttributes alarm_values;

    unsigned long alarm_mask;

    alarm_values.trigger.counter = counter;
    alarm_values.trigger.value_type = valtype;
    alarm_values.trigger.wait_value = testval;
    alarm_values.trigger.test_type = testtype;
    alarm_values.delta = delta;
    alarm_values.events = events;
    alarm_mask = XSyncCACounter|XSyncCAValueType|XSyncCAValue
        |XSyncCATestType|XSyncCADelta|XSyncCAEvents;

    XSyncChangeAlarm(dpy, alarm, alarm_mask, alarm_values);
}


Bool
PredicateProc(dpy, xev, arg)
Display  *dpy;
XEvent   *xev;
char  *arg;
{
    if(xev->type == AlarmNotify)
        return True;
```

```
        else
            return False;
}


void
ExpectAlarmNotify(dpy)
Display *dpy;
{
    XEvent xev;
    XSyncAlarmNotifyEvent *pane;
    char *stuff = (char *)NULL;
    XSyncValue to_do;
    Bool overflow;

    /* Alarm updates automatically: delta is added to wait_value. */
    XIfEvent(dpy, &xev, PredicateProc, stuff);

    pane = (XSyncAlarmNotifyEvent *)&xev;

    /* Determine if request batch needs to catch up. */
    XSyncValueSubtract(&to_do, pane->counter_value,
        pane->alarm_value, &overflow);
    frames_to_do += global_batch +
        XSyncValueLow32(to_do)/XSyncValueLow32(sync_delay);

    /* Send next block of requests. */
    while(frames_to_do)
    {
        DoReDraw(False);
        frames_to_do--;
    }
    return;
}
```

To compile this program, you must include the XSync header file *<X11/extensions/sync.h>* in the source file. You also need to specify the X extension library (*libXext*), the X library (*libX11*), and the math library (*libm*) on the compiler command line. To compile this program when the required libraries are in their standard locations, use the following:

```
% cc -o syncit syncit.c -lXext -lX11 -lm
```

MOTIF PROGRAM

The next program, *xmsync*, uses the Motif toolkit to illustrate synchronization. This program uses a DrawingArea widget to render the graphics and allows wait condition or alarm synchronization to be selected by command line options. When a wait condition or alarm is not specified on the command line, `XtAppAddTimeOut()` is used to keep the rendering operations in pace with the drawing operations. However, the animation does not catch up when the window is moved, mapped or resized. A delay amount can also be specified on the command line, and once again, delay amounts greater than 25 milliseconds are most useful. The number of frames to batch can also be specified on the command line.

Here are some usage examples. To use `XtAppAddTimeOut()` with a delay of 25 milliseconds (instead of a wait condition or alarm):

```
% xmsync -display manray:0 -delay 25
```

To use a wait condition with a delay of 25 milliseconds:

```
% xmsync -display manray:0 -wait -delay 25
```

To use an alarm with a delay of 25 milliseconds and a batch size of 2:

```
% xmsync -display manray:0 -alarm -delay 25 -batch 2
```

This program also uses the `DoSyncInit()` function shown earlier. During execution, the program performs the following operations:

- Initializes the toolkit and display.
- Obtains application resources.
- Creates application widgets.
- If a wait condition or alarm is specified, initializes the SYNC extension, initializes the wait condition or alarm, and loops through the animation using the wait condition or alarm.
- If a wait condition or alarm is not specified, loops through the animation using `XtAppAddTimeOut()`.

```
#ifndef lint
static char sccsid[ ] = "@(#) xmsync.c 1.4 2/20/95";
#endif

#include <stdio.h>
#include <math.h>

#include <X11/Xlib.h>
#include <Xm/XmAll.h>
#include <X11/extensions/sync.h>

#define POINTS 6

typedef struct {
    XPoint points[POINTS];
    XPoint prev_points[POINTS];
} GraphicUnit;
```

```
typedef struct {
    GraphicUnit graphics;
    GC xor_gc;
    Dimension width, height;
    double start_angle;
    Widget work_area;
    Bool winevent;
} Graphic;

String fallback_resources[] =
{
    "*work_area.foreground: tan",
    "*work_area.background: midnightblue",
    NULL
};

typedef struct {
  Bool wait;
  Bool alarm;
  int delay;
  int batch;
  Pixel foreground;
  Pixel background;
} ApplicationData;

static ApplicationData AppData;

static XtResource resources[] = {
    { "wait", "Wait", XmRBoolean, sizeof(Bool),
        XtOffsetOf (ApplicationData, wait),
        XmRString, (caddr_t) "No" },
    { "alarm", "Alarm", XmRBoolean, sizeof(Bool),
        XtOffsetOf (ApplicationData, alarm),
        XmRString, (caddr_t) "No" },
    { "delay", "Delay", XmRInt, sizeof(int),
        XtOffsetOf (ApplicationData, delay),
        XmRString, (caddr_t) "5" },
    { "batch", "Batch", XmRInt, sizeof(int),
        XtOffsetOf (ApplicationData, batch),
        XmRString, (caddr_t)"1" },
    {XmNforeground, XmCForeground, XmRPixel, sizeof (Pixel),
        XtOffsetOf (ApplicationData, foreground),
        XmRString, "tan"},
```

```
        {XmNbackground, XmCBackground, XmRPixel, sizeof (Pixel),
            XtOffsetOf (ApplicationData, background),
            XmRString, "midnightblue"}
};

static XrmOptionDescRec options[] = {
{ "-wait", "*wait", XrmoptionNoArg, "Yes"},
{ "-alarm", "*alarm", XrmoptionNoArg, "Yes"},
{ "-batch", "*batch", XrmoptionSepArg, NULL},
{ "-delay", "*delay", XrmoptionSepArg, NULL},
};

static Bool first_time = True;
static Bool init = True;

char *ProgramName = "unknown_program";
static XtAppContext app_context;
Graphic thestar;

/* Sync Stuff */
static XSyncCounter server_time = None;
static XSyncAlarm    server_alarm = None;
static XSyncWaitCondition cond = None;

static int frames_to_do = 0;
static int AlarmNotify = 0;
static int CounterNotify = 0;

XSyncValue sync_delay;
XSyncValue sync_count;
int sync_major, sync_minor;
int sync_event, sync_error;

/* Forward declarations */
void CreateApplication ();
void DrawCB ();
void InitDraw ();
void DoRedraw();
void DoRotate();
void AlarmNotifyEvent();
void ChangeAlarm();
void DoTimeout();

Bool DoSyncInit();
```

```
Bool AnimWorkProc();

main(argc, argv)
int argc; char **argv;
{
    Widget toplevel;
    Display *dpy;

    ProgramName = argv[0];

    toplevel = XtAppInitialize(&app_context, "XMsync",
        options, XtNumber(options),
        &argc, argv, fallback_resources, NULL, 0);

    dpy = XtDisplay(toplevel);

    XtGetApplicationResources(toplevel,
        (XtPointer)&AppData, resources, XtNumber(resources),
        NULL, 0);

    CreateApplication(toplevel, &thestar);

    if(AppData.wait || AppData.alarm)
    {
        if(AppData.wait)
           AppData.alarm = 0;
        else if(AppData.alarm)
           AppData.wait = 0;

        if(!DoSyncInit(dpy)  )
        {
            XCloseDisplay(dpy);
            exit(1);
        }

        /* Synchronization trigger for XSyncAwait(). */
        if(AppData.wait)
        {
            Bool overflow;

            /* Convert delay to 64 bit value. */
            XSyncIntToValue(&sync_delay, AppData.delay);

            /* Retrieve system counter initial value. */
```

```
        XSyncQueryCounter(dpy, server_time, &sync_count);

        /* Add delay to counter value.*/
        XSyncValueAdd(&sync_count, sync_count, sync_delay, &overflow);

        /* Set wait conditions. */
        cond.trigger.counter = server_time;
        cond.trigger.value_type = XSyncAbsolute;
        cond.trigger.test_type = XSyncPositiveComparison;

        /* Set event threshold to 1 to show any missed deadlines. */
        XSyncIntToValue(&cond.event_threshold, 1);
    }

    /* Synchronization trigger for XSyncAlarmNotify. */
    if(AppData.alarm)
    {
        server_alarm = XSyncCreateAlarm(dpy,
            0L, (XSyncAlarmAttributes *)NULL);
        /* Calculate alarm delta as delay * frames in batch. */
        XSyncIntToValue(&sync_delay, AppData.delay*AppData.batch);

        /* Trigger test value is counter value + wait_value. */
        ChangeAlarm(dpy, server_alarm, server_time, XSyncRelative,
            /* wait_value */ sync_delay, XSyncPositiveComparison,
            /* delta      */ sync_delay, True);
    }
}

InitDraw(&thestar);
XtRealizeWidget(toplevel);
DoRedraw(&thestar);

if(AppData.wait || AppData.alarm)
{
    while(1)
    {
        if(XPending(dpy) || AppData.alarm )
        {
            XEvent xev;

            XtAppNextEvent(app_context, &xev);
            if(xev.type == AlarmNotify)
                AlarmNotifyEvent(&xev);
```

```
                else
                    XtDispatchEvent(&xev);
            }
            if(AppData.wait)
                DoRotate(&thestar);
        }
    }
    else
    {
        XtAppAddTimeOut(app_context, AppData.delay*AppData.batch,
            DoTimeout, &thestar);
        XtAppMainLoop(app_context);
    }
}


void
CreateApplication (parent, graph)
Widget parent;
Graphic *graph;
{
    Widget    main_window;
    Arg       args[5];
    int       n = 0;

    /* Create a MainWindow to contain the drawing area */
    main_window = XmCreateMainWindow (parent, "main_window", NULL, 0);
    XtManageChild(main_window);

    /* Create work_area in MainWindow */
    n = 0;
    XtSetArg(args[n], XmNmarginWidth, 0); n++;
    XtSetArg(args[n], XmNmarginHeight, 0); n++;
    XtSetArg(args[n], XmNwidth, 100);  n++ ;
    XtSetArg(args[n], XmNheight, 100); n++ ;

    graph->work_area = XmCreateDrawingArea(main_window, "work_area",
        args, n);
    XtAddCallback(graph->work_area, XmNexposeCallback, DrawCB,
        (XtPointer)graph);
    XtAddCallback(graph->work_area, XmNresizeCallback, DrawCB,
        (XtPointer)graph);
    XtManageChild(graph->work_area);
}
```

```
static Bool
AnimWorkProc(client_data, id)
XtPointer client_data;
XtWorkProcId id;
{
    Graphic *graph = (Graphic *) client_data;

    graph->winevent = False;
    DoRedraw(graph);

    if (--frames_to_do <= 1)
    {
        XFlush(XtDisplay(graph->work_area) );
        return True;
    }
    return False;
}

static void
DoTimeout(client_data, id)
XtPointer client_data;
XtIntervalId id;
{
    Graphic *graph = (Graphic *) client_data;

    XtAppAddTimeOut(app_context, AppData.delay, DoTimeout, client_data);
    graph->winevent = False;

    DoRedraw(graph);
    XFlush(XtDisplay(graph->work_area));
}

void
DrawCB(w, client_data, call_data)
Widget w;
caddr_t client_data;
caddr_t call_data;
{
    XmDrawingAreaCallbackStruct *dacs =
        (XmDrawingAreaCallbackStruct *) call_data;
    Arg  args[5];
    int n;
    Dimension width, height;
    XSetWindowAttributes xswa;
```

```
        XWindowAttributes xwa;
        Graphic *graph = (Graphic *) client_data;

        switch (dacs->reason)
        {
        case XmCR_EXPOSE:
            if (first_time)
            {
                    XGetWindowAttributes(XtDisplay(w),
                    XtWindow(w), &xwa);
                    graph->width = xwa.width / 2;
                    graph->height = xwa.height / 2;
                    graph->start_angle = 0.0;

                    first_time = False;
                    xswa.bit_gravity = ForgetGravity;
                    XChangeWindowAttributes(XtDisplay(w), XtWindow(w),
                        CWBitGravity, &xswa);
            }
            graph->winevent = True;
            DoRedraw(graph);
            break;
        case XmCR_RESIZE:
            n = 0;
            XtSetArg (args[n], XmNwidth, &width);  n++;
            XtSetArg (args[n], XmNheight, &height);  n++;
            XtGetValues (w, args, n);

            graph->winevent = True;
            graph->width = width/2;
            graph->height = height/2;
            DoRedraw(graph);
            break;
        default:
             break;
        }
}

void
InitDraw(graph)
Graphic *graph;
{
    XGCValues val;
    Arg       args[5];
```

```
    int      n;
    Cardinal i;
    Dimension width, height;
    int      x, y;
    n = 0;

    XtSetArg(args[n], XmNforeground, &val.foreground);  n++;
    XtSetArg(args[n], XmNbackground, &val.background);  n++;
    XtGetValues(graph->work_area, args, n);

    val.foreground = val.foreground ^ val.background;
    val.function = GXxor;
    graph->xor_gc = XtGetGC(graph->work_area,
        GCForeground | GCBackground | GCFunction, &val);
}

void
DoRedraw(graph)
Graphic *graph;
{
    register inti;
    double angle;
    Widget w = graph->work_area;
    if(!init)
    {
        if(graph->winevent)
            XClearWindow(XtDisplay(w), XtWindow(w) );
        else
            XDrawLines(XtDisplay(w), XtWindow(w),
                graph->xor_gc, graph->graphics.prev_points,
                POINTS, CoordModeOrigin);
    }
    graph->start_angle += M_PI / 60.0;
    angle = graph->start_angle;
    for (i=0; i<POINTS; i++)
    {
        graph->graphics.points[i].x =
            graph->width + graph->width * cos(angle);
        graph->graphics.points[i].y =
            graph->height + graph->height * sin(angle);
        graph->graphics.prev_points[i].x = graph->graphics.points[i].x;
        graph->graphics.prev_points[i].y = graph->graphics.points[i].y;
        angle += 4.0 * M_PI / ((double) (POINTS-1));
    }
```

```
        if(init)
            init = False;
        XDrawLines(XtDisplay(w), XtWindow(w),
            graph->xor_gc, graph->graphics.points,
            POINTS, CoordModeOrigin);
    }

    void
    DoRotate(graph)
    Graphic *graph;
    {
        Bool overflow;

        XSync(XtDisplay(graph->work_area), False);

        /* Update wait value. */
        XSyncValueAdd(&sync_count, sync_count, sync_delay, &overflow);
        cond.trigger.wait_value = sync_count;

        /* Block until trigger is True. */
        XSyncAwait(XtDisplay(graph->work_area), &cond, 1);
        /* Calculate and render graphics. */
        DoRedraw(graph);
    }

    void
    ChangeAlarm(dpy, alarm, counter, valtype, testval, testtype, delta, events)
    Display *dpy;
    XSyncAlarm alarm;
    XSyncCounter counter;
    XSyncValue  testval, delta;
    int valtype, testtype, events;
    {
        XSyncAlarmAttributes alarm_values;
        unsigned long alarm_mask;

        alarm_values.trigger.counter = counter;
        alarm_values.trigger.value_type = valtype;
        alarm_values.trigger.wait_value = testval;
        alarm_values.trigger.test_type = testtype;
        alarm_values.delta = delta;
        alarm_values.events = events;
        alarm_mask = XSyncCACounter|XSyncCAValueType|XSyncCAValue
            |XSyncCATestType|XSyncCADelta|XSyncCAEvents;
```

```
        XSyncChangeAlarm(dpy, alarm, alarm_mask, alarm_values);
}


void
AlarmNotifyEvent(xev)
XEvent  *xev;
{
    XSyncAlarmNotifyEvent *pane = (XSyncAlarmNotifyEvent *)xev;
    XSyncValue to_do;
    Bool overflow;
    XtWorkProcId workID;

    /* Determine if request batch needs to catch up. */
    XSyncValueSubtract(&to_do, pane->counter_value,
        pane->alarm_value, &overflow);
    frames_to_do += AppData.batch +
        XSyncValueLow32(to_do)/XSyncValueLow32(sync_delay);

    if(frames_to_do > 0)
        workID = XtAppAddWorkProc(app_context, AnimWorkProc, &thestar);
}
```

To compile this program, you must include the XSync header file *<X11/extensions/sync.h>* in the source file. You also need to specify the X extension library (*libXext*), the Motif library (*libXm*), the X Toolkit library (*libXt*), the X library (*libX11*), and the math library (*libm*) on the compiler command line. To compile this program when the required libraries are in their standard locations, enter the following:

```
% cc -o xmsync xmsync.c -lXext -lXm -lXt -lX11 -lm
```

REFERENCES

[Glauert94] Tim Glauert, Dave Carver, et al. X Synchronization Extension. X Version 11. Release 6.

XSyncAwait

Wait on a condition.

SYNOPSIS

```
#include <X11/extensions/sync.h>

Status XSyncAwait(
    Display             *dpy,
    XSyncWaitCondition *wait_list,
    int                 n_conditions )
```

ARGUMENTS

dpy
Specifies a connection to an X server.

wait_list
Specifies the list of conditions to wait for.

n_conditions
Specifies the number of conditions in the list.

RETURNS

Returns **False** if *dpy* does not support the SYNC extension; otherwise returns **True**.

DESCRIPTION

XSyncAwait() causes the client to block until one or more of the triggers in *wait_list* become **True**. Before the client blocks, each trigger in the list is initialized, and its test value is calculated. When a trigger in the list becomes **True**, the client unblocks, and the X server's processing of the client's requests continues with the first request following XSyncAwait(). As the client unblocks, each trigger in *wait_list* is checked to see if an **XSyncCounterNotify** event should be generated.

STRUCTURES

```
typedef struct _XSyncValue {
    int hi;
    unsigned int lo;
} XSyncValue;

typedef struct {
    XSyncCounter counter;
    XSyncValueType value_type;
    XSyncValue wait_value;
    XSyncTestType test_type;
} XSyncTrigger;
```

The test value of a trigger is calculated when the trigger is initialized. If value_type is XSyncAbsolute, the trigger test value is simply wait_value. If value_type is XSyncRelative, the test value is the value of counter plus wait_value.

The following describes the possible values of test_type and the conditions under which the trigger test value is True:

XSyncPositiveTransition

   When counter changes from a value less than the test value to a value greater than or equal to the test value.

XSyncNegativeTransition

   When counter changes from a value greater than the test value to a value less than or equal to the test value.

XSyncPositiveComparison

   When counter is greater than or equal to the test value.

XSyncNegativeComparison

   When counter is less than or equal to the test value.

A trigger with a counter of None is always True.

```
typedef struct {
      XSyncTrigger trigger;
      XSyncValue event_threshold;
} XSyncWaitCondition;
```

Whether or not an XSyncCounterNotify event is generated is determined by subtracting the test value from the counter value. For positive conditions, an event is generated when the difference is greater and or equal to event_threshold. For negative conditions, an event is generated when the difference is less than or equal to event_threshold.

```
typedef struct {
      int type;                /* event base + XSyncCounterNotify */
      unsigned long serial;    /* # of last request processed by server */
      Bool send_event;         /* true if this came from a SendEvent request */
      Display *display;        /* Display the event was read from */
      XSyncCounter counter;    /* counter involved in await */
      XSyncValue wait_value;   /* value being waited for */
      XSyncValue counter_value; /* counter value when this event was sent */
      Time time;               /* milliseconds */
      int count;               /* how many more events to come */
      Bool destroyed;          /* True if counter was destroyed */
} XSyncCounterNotifyEvent;
```

BadCounter

A specified counter does not exist on the display.

BadValue

A specified value is invalid, or *wait_list* is empty.

SEE ALSO

XSyncCreateCounter()
XSyncChangeCounter()
XSyncSetCounter()
XSyncDestroyCounter()

XSyncChangeAlarm

Change an alarm.

SYNOPSIS

```
#include <X11/extensions/sync.h>

Status XSyncChangeAlarm(
    Display             *dpy,
    XSyncAlarm          alarm,
    unsigned long       alarm_mask,
    XSyncAlarmAttributes *alarm_values )
```

ARGUMENTS

dpy

> Specifies a connection to an X server.

alarm

> Specifies the alarm.

alarm_mask

> Specifies which alarm attributes to set.

alarm_values

> Specifies the alarm attributes.

RETURNS

Returns `False` if *dpy* does not support the SYNC extension; otherwise returns `True`.

DESCRIPTION

XSyncChangeAlarm() changes the specified *alarm* to the attributes *alarm_mask* and *alarm_values*. All of the parameters specified for XSyncCreateAlarm() can be changed using this function. When the alarm parameters change, the alarm trigger re-initializes, and an XSyncAlarmNotify event is generated when the alarm trigger becomes `True`.

ERRORS

BadAlarm

> The specified alarm does not exist on the display.

BadCounter

> The specified counter does not exist on the display.

BadMatch

> A specified alarm attribute is invalid.

`BadValue`

A specified alarm attribute value is invalid.

SEE ALSO

`XSyncCreateAlarm()`

XSyncChangeCounter

Change the value of a client counter.

SYNOPSIS

```
#include <X11/extensions/sync.h>

Status XSyncChangeCounter(
    Display       *dpy,
    XSyncCounter  counter,
    XSyncValue     value )
```

ARGUMENTS

dpy
>   Specifies a connection to an X server.

counter
>   Specifies the counter.

value
>   Specifies the amount to add to the current counter value.

RETURNS

Returns False if dpy does not support the SYNC extension; otherwise returns True.

DESCRIPTION

XSyncChangeCounter() adds the value of value to the current value of counter. An XSyncAlarmNotify event is generated for any alarm specifying the counter when the alarm trigger becomes True as the result of the new counter value. Any clients that have called XSyncAwait() on the counter and are currently blocking become unblocked if the new counter value results in the trigger becoming True.

STRUCTURES

```
typedef struct _XSyncValue {
    int hi;
    unsigned int lo;
} XSyncValue;
```

ERRORS

BadCounter
>   The specified counter does not exist on the display.

BadAccess
>   The specified counter is a system counter.

`BadValue`
    The new counter value is outside the valid range.

SEE ALSO

`XSyncCreateCounter()`
`XSyncSetCounter()`
`XSyncAwait()`

XSyncCreateAlarm

Create an alarm.

SYNOPSIS

```
#include <X11/extensions/sync.h>

XSyncAlarm XSyncCreateAlarm(
    Display             *dpy,
    unsigned long       alarm_mask,
    XSyncAlarmAttributes *alarm_values )
```

ARGUMENTS

dpy

Specifies a connection to an X server.

alarm_mask

Specifies which alarm attributes to set.

alarm_values

Specifies the alarm attributes.

RETURNS

Returns the resource ID of the created alarm. Returns **False** if *dpy* does not support the SYNC extension.

DESCRIPTION

XSyncCreateAlarm() creates an alarm on the specified *dpy* with the initialized attributes *alarm_mask* and *alarm_values*. The resource ID of the created alarm, which uniquely identifies the alarm, is returned on success.

The relationship between *alarm_values* fields and *alarm_mask* values are as follows:

Field Name	Alarm Mask
trigger.counter	XSyncACounter
trigger.value_type	XSyncAValueType
trigger.wait_value	XSyncAValue
trigger.test_type	XSyncATestType
delta	XSyncADelta
events	XSyncAEvents
state	Cannot be set by client

When the alarm is initialized, the trigger's test value is calculated. The alarm is initialized to an active state unless the trigger **counter** is **None**, in which case, the alarm is initialized to an inactive state. When the test value of the trigger becomes `True`, an `XSyncA-larmNotify` is generated, and the alarm is updated by adding `delta` to `wait_value`, and re-initializing the alarm. The `events` field in either enables or disables delivery of `XSyncAlarmNotify` events to the client. The state field value corresponds to the state field in the `XSyncAlarmNotify` event.

STRUCTURES

```
typedef struct _XSyncValue {
    int hi;
    unsigned int lo;
} XSyncValue;

typedef struct {
    XSyncCounter counter;
    XSyncValueType value_type;
    XSyncValue wait_value;
    XSyncTestType test_type;
} XSyncTrigger;
```

The test value of a trigger is calculated when the trigger is initialized. If `value_type` is `XSyncAbsolute`, the trigger test value is simply `wait_value`. If `value_type` is `XSyncRelative`, the test value is the value of `counter` plus `wait_value`.

The following describes the possible values of `test_type` and the conditions under which the trigger test value is `True`:

XSyncPositiveTransition

When `counter` changes from a value less than the test value to a value greater than or equal to the test value.

XSyncNegativeTransition

When `counter` changes from a value greater than the test value to a value less than or equal to the test value.

XSyncPositiveComparison

When `counter` is greater than or equal to the test value.

XSyncNegativeComparison

When `counter` is less than or equal to the test value.

A trigger with a `counter` of `None` is always `True`.

```
typedef struct {
    XSyncTrigger trigger;
    XSyncValue  delta;
    Bool events;
    XSyncAlarmState state;
} XSyncAlarmAttributes;
```

```
typedef struct {
    int type;                 /* event base + XSyncAlarmNotify */
    unsigned long serial;     /* # of last request processed by server */
    Bool send_event;          /* true if this came from a SendEvent request */
    Display *display;         /* Display the event was read from */
    XSyncAlarm alarm;         /* alarm that triggered */
    XSyncValue counter_value; /* value that triggered the alarm */
    XSyncValue alarm_value;   /* test  value of trigger in alarm */
    Time time;                /* milliseconds */
    XSyncAlarmState state;    /* new state of alarm */
} XSyncAlarmNotifyEvent;
```

ERRORS

BadCounter
> The specified counter does not exist on the display.

BadMatch
> A specified alarm attribute is invalid.

BadValue
> A specified alarm attribute value is invalid.

SEE ALSO

XSyncChangeAlarm()
XSyncDestroyAlarm()

XSyncCreateCounter

Create a client counter.

SYNOPSIS

```
#include <X11/extensions/sync.h>

XSyncCounter XSyncCreateCounter(
    Display    *dpy,
    XSyncValue    initial_value )
```

ARGUMENTS

dpy
Specifies a connection to an X server.

initial_value
Specifies the initial value of the counter.

RETURNS

Returns the resource ID of the created counter. Returns **None** if *dpy* does not support the SYNC extension.

DESCRIPTION

XSyncCreateCounter() creates a client counter on the specified *dpy* with the initial value of *initial_value*. The resource ID of the created counter, which uniquely identifies the counter, is returned on success.

STRUCTURES

```
typedef struct _XSyncValue {
    int hi;
    unsigned int lo;
} XSyncValue;
```

SEE ALSO

XSyncDestroyCounter()
XSyncSetCounter()
XSyncChangeCounter()

XSyncDestroyAlarm

Destroy an alarm.

SYNOPSIS

```
#include <X11/extensions/sync.h>

Status XSyncDestroyAlarm(
    Display    *dpy,
    XSyncAlarm    alarm )
```

ARGUMENTS

dpy
> Specifies a connection to an X server.

alarm
> Specifies the alarm.

RETURNS

Returns `False` if *dpy* does not support the SYNC extension; otherwise returns `True`.

DESCRIPTION

XSyncDestroyAlarm() destroys the specified *alarm*. When the alarm is destroyed, an XSyncAlarmNotify event is generated with the state field in the event set to XSyncA-larmDestroyed.

ERRORS

BadAlarm
> The specified alarm does not exist on the display.

SEE ALSO

XSyncCreateAlarm()
XSyncChangeAlarm()

XSyncDestroyCounter

Destroy a client counter.

SYNOPSIS

```
#include <X11/extensions/sync.h>

Status
XSyncDestroyCounter(
    Display        *dpy,
    XSyncCounter    counter )
```

ARGUMENTS

dpy
> Specifies a connection to an X server.

counter
> Specifies the counter.

RETURNS

Returns `False` if *dpy* does not support the SYNC extension; otherwise returns `True`.

DESCRIPTION

XSyncDestroyCounter() destroys the specified *counter* and sets the `trigger.counter` field for all triggers that have specified the counter to `None`.

Any clients that have called `XSyncAwait()` on the counter and are currently blocking become unblocked and are sent a `XSyncCounterNotify` event with the `destroyed` field set to `True`. Any alarms specifying the counter become inactive, and an `XSyncAlarmNotify` event is generated with the `state` field in the event set to `XSyncAlarmInactive`.

ERRORS

`BadCounter`
> The specified counter does not exist on the display.

`BadAccess`
> The specified counter is a system counter.

SEE ALSO

XSyncAwait()
XSyncCreateCounter()

XSyncFreeSystemCounterList

Free a list of system counters.

Synopsis

```
#include <X11/extensions/sync.h>

void XSyncFreeSystemCounterList(
    Display            *dpy,
    XSyncSystemCounter *list )
```

Arguments

dpy
> Specifies a connection to an X server.

list
> Specifies the system counter list.

Description

XSyncFreeSystemCounterList() is the means for freeing the memory associated with the list returned by XSyncListSystemCounters().

Structures

```
typedef struct _XSyncSystemCounter {
    char *name;
    XSyncCounter counter;
    XSyncValue resolution;
} XSyncSystemCounter;
```

See Also

XSyncListSystemCounters()

XSyncGetPriority

Retrieve client's scheduling priority.

SYNOPSIS

```
#include <X11/extensions/sync.h>

Status XSyncGetPriority(
    Display *dpy,
    XID       client_resource_id,
    int       *return_priority)
```

ARGUMENTS

dpy

> Specifies a connection to an X server.

client_resource_id

> Identifies the client that created the resource ID.

return_priority

> Returns the scheduling priority of the client.

RETURNS

Returns `False` if *dpy* does not support the SYNC extension; otherwise returns `True`.

DESCRIPTION

XSyncGetPriority() retrieves the scheduling priority of the client that created the resource ID *client_resource_id*. If *client_resource_id* is None, the scheduling priority of the client issuing the request is returned.

ERRORS

BadMatch

> The specified resource ID does not name an existing resource.

SEE ALSO

XSyncSetPriority()

XSyncInitialize

Determine the version of the SYNC extension.

SYNOPSIS

```
#include <X11/extensions/sync.h>

Status XSyncInitialize(
     Display  *dpy,
     int       *major_version,
     int        *minor_version)
```

ARGUMENTS

dpy

Specifies a connection to an X server.

major_version

Returns the major version number of the extension supported by the display.

minor_version

Returns the minor version number of the extension supported by the display.

RETURNS

Returns **True** if the XSync library is compatible with the server. Returns **False** if the server does not support the SYNC extension or if the server and the library protocol versions are incompatible.

DESCRIPTION

XSyncInitialize() is the means for determining the SYNC protocol version supported by server. XSyncQueryExtension() is the only XSync function that may be called before XSyncInitialize(). Given that each revision of the protocol is assigned a version number and may change over time, this function ensures that the server version of SYNC is usable by the client. The current SYNC version is 3.0. This function would therefore return 3 as the major version and 0 as the minor version.

SEE ALSO

XSyncQueryExtension()

XSyncListSystemCounters

List the system counters.

SYNOPSIS

```
#include <X11/extensions/sync.h>

XSyncSystemCounter * XSyncListSystemCounters(
    Display  *dpy,
    int       *n_counters_return )
```

ARGUMENTS

dpy

Specifies a connection to an X server.

`n_counters_return`

Returns the number of system counters currently available in *dpy*.

RETURNS

Returns the list of all available system counters. Returns **NULL** if *dpy* does not support the SYNC extension.

DESCRIPTION

XSyncListSystemCounters() is the means for determining what system counters are currently available in an X server. All servers that implement the SYNC extension are guaranteed to have at least one system counter: **SERVERTIME**. **SERVERTIME** counts in milliseconds from an arbitrary starting point. The least significant 32 bits of the **SERVERTIME** value correspond to the `time` field in events and requests.

Each system counter has a `name` field that is the textual name that identifies the counter, a `counter` field that is the resource ID of the counter, and a `resolution` field that approximates the step size of the counter.

STRUCTURES

```
typedef struct _XSyncValue {
    int hi;
    unsigned int lo;
} XSyncValue;

typedef struct _XSyncSystemCounter {
    char *name;
    XSyncCounter counter;
    XSyncValue resolution;
} XSyncSystemCounter;
```

SEE ALSO

`XSyncFreeSystemCounters()`

XSyncQueryAlarm

Query alarm attributes.

SYNOPSIS

```
#include <X11/extensions/sync.h>

Status XSyncQueryAlarm(
    Display             *dpy,
    XSyncAlarm          alarm,
    XSyncAlarmAttributes *values_return )
```

ARGUMENTS

dpy

Specifies a connection to an X server.

alarm

Specifies the alarm.

value_return

Returns the current *alarm* attributes.

RETURNS

Returns **False** if *dpy* does not support the SYNC extension; otherwise returns **True**.

DESCRIPTION

XSyncQueryAlarm() retrieves the current attributes of *alarm*.

STRUCTURES

```
typedef struct {
    XSyncTrigger trigger;
    XSyncValue  delta;
    Bool events;
    XSyncAlarmState state;
} XSyncAlarmAttributes;
```

ERRORS

BadAlarm

The specified alarm does not exist on the display.

SEE ALSO

XSyncCreateAlarm()
XSyncChangeAlarm()

XSyncQueryCounter

Query counter value.

SYNOPSIS

```
#include <X11/extensions/sync.h>

Status XSyncQueryCounter(
    Display       *dpy,
    XSyncCounter   counter,
    XSyncValue     *value_return )
```

ARGUMENTS

dpy
> Specifies a connection to an X server.

counter
> Specifies the counter.

value_return
> Returns the current *counter* value.

RETURNS

Returns **False** if *dpy* does not support the SYNC extension; otherwise returns **True**.

DESCRIPTION

XSyncQueryCounter() retrieves the current value of *counter*.

STRUCTURES

```
typedef struct _XSyncValue {
    int hi;
    unsigned int lo;
} XSyncValue;
```

ERRORS

BadCounter
> The specified counter does not exist on the display.

SEE ALSO

XSyncCreateCounter()
XSyncSetCounter()
XSyncChangeCounter()
XSyncDestroyCounter()

XSyncQueryExtension

Determine support for the SYNC extension.

SYNOPSIS

```
#include <X11/extensions/sync.h>

Status XSyncQueryExtension(
    Display *dpy,
    int     *first_event,
    int      *first_error,
```

ARGUMENTS

dpy

Specifies a connection to an X server.

first_event

Returns the event code that is set to the number of the first SYNC extension event.

first_error

Returns the error code that is set to the error number of the first SYNC error.

RETURNS

Returns **True** if the XSync extension is available on the server; otherwise returns **False**.

DESCRIPTION

XSyncQueryExtension() is the primary means for determining whether SYNC exists in a server. Typically, this is the first XSync function called by a program. Its return status indicates whether SYNC is available.

Since the event and error codes of extensions are determined by the server, an application must obtain the base event code and base error code from the server in order to form the SYNC event types and error codes. The SYNC event types and error codes are formed by adding the base code returned by this function to the constants defined in *X11/extensions/ sync.h*.

SEE ALSO

XSyncInitialize()

XSyncSetCounter

Set the value of a client counter.

```
#include <X11/extensions/sync.h>

Status XSyncSetCounter(
    Display       *dpy,
    XSyncCounter  counter,
    XSyncValue    value )
```

ARGUMENTS

dpy
> Specifies a connection to an X server.

counter
> Specifies the counter.

new_value
> Specifies the counter value.

RETURNS

Returns `False` if *dpy* does not support the SYNC extension; otherwise returns `True`.

DESCRIPTION

`XSyncSetCounter()` sets the value of *counter* to *value*. An `XSyncAlarmNotify` event is generated for any alarm specifying the counter when the alarm trigger becomes `True` as the result of the new counter value. Any clients that have called `XSyncAwait()` on the counter and are currently blocking become unblocked if the new counter value results in the trigger becoming `True`.

STRUCTURES

```
typedef struct _XSyncValue {
    int hi;
    unsigned int lo;
} XSyncValue;
```

ERRORS

`BadCounter`
> The specified counter does not exist on the display.

`BadAccess`
> The specified counter is a system counter.

```
XSyncCreateCounter()
XSyncChangeCounter()
XSyncAwait()
```

XSyncSetPriority

Change client's scheduling priority.

SYNOPSIS

```
#include <X11/extensions/sync.h>

Status XSyncSetPriority(
    Display *dpy,
    XID      client_resource_id,
    int      priority)
```

ARGUMENTS

dpy
>   Specifies a connection to an X server.

client_resource_id
>   Identifies the client that created the specified resource ID.

return_priority
>   Specifies the scheduling priority of the client.

RETURNS

Returns `False` if *dpy* does not support the SYNC extension; otherwise returns `True`.

DESCRIPTION

XSyncSetPriority() changes the scheduling priority of the client that created the resource ID *client_resource_id*. If *client_resource_id* is None, the scheduling priority of the client issuing the request is changed. A client's scheduling priority is set to 0 (zero) when it makes its initial connection to the X server. The effect of different client priorities is implementation-dependent. However, typically, the requests of higher priority clients are executed before those of lower priority clients. Window managers are expected to be the primary users of XSyncSetPriority(). High priority clients (scheduling priority greater than zero) are polled before other clients, and their pending requests are executed before another client can run. Normal priority clients (scheduling priority equal to zero) follow the normal round-robin scheduling mechanism. Low priority clients (scheduling priority less than zero) are polled after each batch of requests is executed and can run only when no other clients have pending requests.

ERRORS

BadMatch
>   The specified resource ID does not name an existing resource.

SEE ALSO

XSyncGetPriority()

Events provided by extension.

SYNOPSIS

```
#include <X11/extensions/sync.h>

typedef struct {
    int type;
    unsigned long serial;
    Bool send_event;
    Display *display
    XSyncCounter counter;
    XSyncValue wait_value;
    XSyncValue counter_value;
    Time time;
    int count;
    Bool destroyed;
} XSyncCounterNotifyEvent;

typedef struct {
    int type;
    unsigned long serial;
    Bool send_event;
    Display *display;
    XSyncAlarm alarm;
    XSyncValue counter_value;
    XSyncValue alarm_value;
    Time time;
    XSyncAlarmState state;
} XSyncAlarmNotifyEvent;
```

DESCRIPTION

The `XSyncCounterNotify` event can be generated when a client unblocks after an `XSyncAwait()` request. The event fields to note are: `counter`, the counter for the event, `wait_value`, the test value of the trigger, `counter_value`, the actual value of the counter, *destroyed*, which is `True` if the counter was destroyed, and `time`, the time of the event.

The `XSyncAlarmNotify` is generated when an alarm trigger becomes `True`. The event fields to note are: `alarm`, the alarm for the event, `alarm_value`, the test value for the trigger in the alarm, `counter_value`, the actual value of the counter when it triggers, `state`, the state of the alarm after an update, and `time`, the time of the event.

STRUCTURES

```
typedef struct _XSyncValue {
    int hi;
    unsigned int lo;
} XSyncValue;

typedef struct _XSyncSystemCounter {
    char *name;
    XSyncCounter counter;
    XSyncValue resolution;
} XSyncSystemCounter;
```

SEE ALSO

```
XSyncFreeSystemCounters()
```

XSync 64-Bit Procedures

Procedures to manipulate 64-bit values.

SYNOPSIS

```
#include <X11/extensions/sync.h>

void XSyncIntToValue(
    XSyncValue *pv,
    int i )

void XSyncIntsToValue(
    XSyncValue *pv,
    unsigned int low,
    int high )

Bool XSyncValueGreaterThan(
    XSyncValue a,
    XSyncValue b )

Bool XSyncValueLessThan(
    XSyncValue a,
    XSyncValue b )

Bool XSyncValueGreaterThanOrEqual(
    XSyncValue a,
    XSyncValue b )

Bool XSyncValueLessThanOrEqual(
    XSyncValue a,
    XSyncValue b )

Bool XSyncValueEqual(
    XSyncValue a,
    XSyncValue b )

Bool XSyncValueIsNegative(
    XSyncValue v )

Bool XSyncValueIsPositive(
    XSyncValue v )

Bool XSyncValueIsZero(
    XSyncValue v )
```

```
unsigned int XSyncValueLow32(
    XSyncValue v )

int XSyncValueHigh32(
    XSyncValue v )

void XSyncValueAdd(
    XSyncValue *presult,
    XSyncValue a,
    XSyncValue b,
    int* poverflow )

void XSyncValueSubtract(
    XSyncValue *presult,
    XSyncValue a,
    XSyncValue b,
    int* poverflow )

void XSyncMaxValue(
    XSyncValue* pv )

void XSyncMinValue(
    XSyncValue* pv )
```

DESCRIPTION

Since counter, trigger, and wait condition parameters require 64-bit values, utility procedures are provided as part of the XSync interface to convert integer values to 64-bit values, compare 64-bit values, and perform arithmetic operations on 64-bit values. These procedures are client-side operations; they send no protocol request.

XSyncIntToValue()
    Converts int *i* to XSyncValue and stores value in *pv*.

XSyncIntsToValue()
    Stores *low* in low 32 bits and *high* in high 32 bits of *pv*.

XSyncValueGreaterThan()
    Returns True if *a* is greater than *b*, otherwise returns False.

XSyncValueLessThan()
    Returns True if *a* is less than *b*, otherwise returns False.

XSyncValueGreaterThanOrEqual()
    Returns True if *a* is greater than or equal to *b*, otherwise returns False.

`XSyncValueLessThanOrEqual()`
> Returns True if *a* is less than or equal to *b*, otherwise returns False.

`XSyncValueEqual()`
> Returns True if *a* is equal to *b*, otherwise returns False.

`XSyncValueIsNegative()`
> Returns True if *v* is negative, otherwise returns False.

`XSyncValueIsPositive()`
> Returns True if *v* is positive, otherwise returns False.

`XSyncValueIsZero()`
> Returns True if *v* is zero, otherwise returns False.

`XSyncValueLow32()`
> Returns the low 32 bits of *v*.

`XSyncValueHigh32()`
> Returns the high 32 bits of *v*.

`XSyncValueAdd()`
> Adds *a* to *b* and stores result in *pv*. If the result cannot fit in 64 bits, *poverflow* is set to True, else it is False.

`XSyncValueSubtract()`
> Subtracts *a* from *b* and stores result in *pv*. If the result cannot fit in 64 bits, *poverflow* is set to True, else it is False.

`XSyncMaxValue()`
> Set *pv* to the maximum 64-bit value.

`XSyncMinValue()`
> Set *pv* to the minimum 64-bit value.

STRUCTURES

```
typedef struct _XSyncValue {
    int hi;
    unsigned int lo;
} XSyncValue;
```

ISSUE 0: FALL 1991

BACK ISSUES OF THE X RESOURCE

ISSUE 1: WINTER 1992

PROCEEDINGS
6TH ANNUAL X TECHNICAL CONFERENCE

BACK ISSUES OF THE X RESOURCE

ISSUE 2: SPRING 1992

BACK ISSUES OF THE X RESOURCE

ISSUE 3: SUMMER 1992

BACK ISSUES OF THE X RESOURCE

ISSUE 4: FALL 1992

ISSUE 5: WINTER 1993

BACK ISSUES OF THE X RESOURCE

ISSUE 6: SPRING 1993

BACK ISSUES OF THE X RESOURCE

ISSUE 7: SUMMER 1993

BACK ISSUES OF THE X RESOURCE

ISSUE 8: FALL 1993

BACK ISSUES OF THE X RESOURCE

ISSUE 9: WINTER 1994

BACK ISSUES OF THE X RESOURCE

ISSUE 10: SPRING 1994

BACK ISSUES OF THE X RESOURCE

ISSUE 11: SUMMER 1994

BACK ISSUES OF THE X RESOURCE

ISSUE 12: FALL 1994

Back Issues of the X Resource

Issue 13: Winter 1995

Proceedings, 9th Annual X Technical Conference

BACK ISSUES OF THE X RESOURCE

ISSUE 14: SPRING 1995

BACK ISSUES OF THE X RESOURCE

ISSUE 15: SUMMER 1995